Give me a BOOST

10 YEARS. 10 WOMEN.
ONE PROMISE TO RISE TOGETHER

Luly B. Carreras ✦ Luly Cordoba ✦ Caroline de Posada
Barbie Garcia ✦ Eva Gonzalez ✦ Dr. Betsy Guerra
Mei Jorge ✦ Gilza Fort Martinez, LMFT ✦ Daniela Mounts
Maitte Penalver ✦ Shannon Summerville-Interian

Copyright © 2024 by Soulfully Aligned Publishing.

ISBN: 979-8-9890749-8-3

All rights reserved.

This publication may only be reproduced, stored, or transmitted with prior written permission from the copyright owner or under licenses issued by the Copyright Licensing Agency for reprographic reproduction. For inquiries outside these terms, contact the publisher.

No part of this publication may be reproduced, distributed, or stored without prior consent, except for brief quotes used in reviews or other non-commercial uses allowed by copyright law.

The author does not provide medical advice or prescribe treatments. The content is intended to offer information to support your well-being journey. If you choose to use the information, the authors assume no responsibility for your actions. Always consult a physician before making any health decisions.

Soulfully Aligned Publishing

DEDICATION

This book is dedicated to you: the woman who is listening to the whispers and knows there's more: more courage, more clarity, more opportunity, more joy, more YOU.

You feel it. You've always known it.

This book is your reminder that you are worthy of it all.

It's your nudge to take the leap, your permission slip to say yes, and your spark to create something bigger than yourself.

Because saying yes to the BOOST isn't just about saying yes to you, it's about the ripple you'll create in your work, your family, your community, and the world.

Here's to leading, rising, and BOOSTING!

Give Me A Boost

TABLE OF
CONTENTS

Dedication iii

Foreword by Maru Macias Carreras vii

Introduction by Luly B. Carreras 1

Chapter 1: When God Calls You for More: How Dare You Not Live Your Purpose Today? by Betsy Guerra, PhD 7

Chapter 2: From Stuck to Starting: Re-Discovering Your Voice in Business by Gilza Fort Martinez, LMFT 23

Chapter 3: Let Go of Your Past, Trust in Your Future by Maitte Penalver 39

Chapter 4: Guided by Faith – Empowered to Plan by Eva Gonzalez 53

Chapter 5: Widowed but not Broken A Mother's Journey to Community, Strength, and a New Calling by Luly Cordoba 69

Chapter 6: Finding Her Light Again and Shining Brighter than Ever by Barbie Garcia 85

Chapter 7: From Trauma to Triumph: The Power of Awareness and Healing in Community by Daniela Mounts 97

Chapter 8: Styled For More: A Woman's Journey of Survival, Awakening, And Power by Mei Jorge 111

Chapter 9: From Chalkboard to Passport: Women Entrepreneurs Unite by Shannon Summerville-Interian 127

Chapter 10: Going at Your Own Pace: For the Woman Who Feels Behind but Is Right on Time by Caroline de Posada 141

Acknowledgements 153

Thank You 157

FOREWORD
BY MARU MACIAS CARRERAS

This isn't a book about one woman. It's a tribute to many. As I read the stories these women so bravely shared, I realized this book is an invitation to all of us to witness, connect, and remember our own journeys. But these women have all come together because of one woman.

To many, she is the founder of the community, BOOST. To me, she is my firstborn daughter, the little girl I watched blossom into a woman. From the moment *my Luly* was born, we knew she was *different.* She had a light in her: bright, bold, and at times, fiery. We used to sing *"You Light Up My Life"* to her as a baby, and even then, we could sense that her light came with purpose.

She saw in people what others didn't. No one was a stranger. Whether it was helping an elderly woman in the store or making sure the quiet child got included at recess, Luly moved through the world with her heart out front. As she grew, so did her conviction. She stood up for what she believed in, even when it got her in trouble.

By the time she entered the business world, Luly was prepared: smart, capable, and full of fire. She built a successful marketing agency while integrating motherhood, always centering her boys. But even at the height of her success, something was missing. For her, fulfillment didn't come from the money or the milestones, it came from service.

So, when she shared with me that she wanted to shut down the agency and start something new—something built to support women—I saw that same clarity in her eyes I'd seen since she was little. The world didn't need another business from Luly. It needed her purpose. And she was ready to share it.

That purpose became BOOST, and this book is a celebration of what it helped SPARK. Luly set out to light the world on fire, to set a fire under every woman who wanted to succeed. She showed that you are not an island, that you cannot isolate yourself, and that you cannot walk alone. Instead, you seek others, seek support, and create a community of positive, supporting women. With that in mind, she created BOOST!

I am beyond proud of the community that Luly has created. I am in awe of the stories I hear from the women she has empowered to meet their abilities, gifts, and potential. These women give to each other and receive from each other, lifting one another to possibilities never thought attainable. The love they share, the boldness they learn, and the willingness to lead or follow as needed is best appreciated by reading the stories of a few in this book who have experienced the BOOSTIE EFFECT.

They all have one thing in common: they are part of this community that uplifted them when they most needed it, made them resilient and irrepressible, and instilled shared values and commitments.

The ten women who share their stories in this book are shining examples of BOOST. They have endured unimaginable challenges. They have made brave choices. They have rebuilt themselves with courage and humility, which they now share with others. All ten stories have a central theme: the quiet power, the strength that comes when women walk alongside one another and give each other a BOOST!

To these ten amazing women—BOOSTIES—I say thank you. I love, admire, and respect each one of you. I deeply appreciate you and love that you are part of my daughter's business, family, and community.

To the reader, you may not know these fabulous women yet, but by the end of this book, you will love them, admire them, and respect them too. You will find, as I have, that their voices will stay with you and touch some part of your life. They speak to something deeper, showing what you can become when you stop trying to carry your load alone.

Give Me A Boost

✦ x ✦

INTRODUCTION
BY LULY B. CARRERAS

We didn't always climb alone. When we were little, asking for a BOOST came naturally. A BOOST to reach the drinking fountain. A BOOST to peek over the counter at the ice cream shop. A BOOST onto the swings, out of the pool, and up to the monkey bars.

We never hesitated. We didn't question if it was too much to ask. We simply knew when we needed help, and we trusted someone would be there. We didn't overthink it or feel guilty. We just reached up, believing we were worthy of the lift.

But somewhere along the way, that changed. The world began to whisper that strength meant doing everything alone. So we stopped asking. We stopped receiving. We learned to push through, even when we were barely holding on. Asking for help became a weakness, a burden, a failure. And with that belief carved into us, we carried our weight in silence, holding everything together, even as it quietly broke us inside.

But the truth is, **we were never meant to do life alone.** Deep down, I've known that since childhood. Community and connection have always been part of my story. At first, there were playground boosts. Later, it was in the hardest seasons of my life, when I needed more than I thought I could ever ask for.

When I walked away from Chispa Marketing, a thriving marketing agency on the brink of hitting a million dollars in revenue, and followed my intuition to create Luly B, Inc., a business that supports women who desire a business and a life of significance.

When I faced infidelity in a 20-year marriage and walked through the devastation of divorce. When the global pandemic slammed into my business and family like a series of gut punches. When I lost my father, my hero, my anchor, my person. When I found the courage to open my heart again, which resulted in finding my soulmate and life partner. When I became a *"bird launcher"* (because I refuse to call myself an empty nester) and embraced the bittersweet beauty of this new season of my family's life. When I returned to my purpose with boldness, carrying a fire that felt brand new.

I've learned that true strength isn't about doing it all. It's about allowing yourself to be held, to be seen, and to be supported. So many of my biggest wins and proudest triumphs have come from asking for a BOOST: making a phone call, sending an email, or asking for help, whether it's to watch my children, sit with me for a good cry, show up at an event, talk through an opportunity or challenge, proofread my work, hold me accountable to my wellness choices, or give me

Introduction

feedback on my next big project. I've been brave enough to ask, and I've kept my heart open to receive, while also being open to the possibility of being declined.

We often say that in giving, we receive. I also believe that in receiving, we give. When we open ourselves up to receive, we allow others to express love and gratitude. Receiving becomes an act of grace. This is the legacy I hope to be remembered for and the message I hope blesses you. Because receiving is not a weakness; it is grace, it is wisdom. It is how we grow, how we rise, and how we love.

And while I didn't always have the language for it, I've been building community since I was three years old. Whether it was inviting the new kid at school to play or speaking up for someone who didn't have a seat at the table, I've always been drawn to connection. It wasn't just about gathering people, but about creating spaces where others feel seen, heard, and valued. Over the years, that calling became both my career and my life's work.

Ten years ago, out of my own journey of saying "yes" to support, both in business and in life, I created a coaching experience called BOOST. At first, it was designed for heart-centered, impact-driven, family-loving women who wanted to grow their businesses with strategy, soul, and support. But almost immediately, it became something more. Much more.

BOOST became a sacred container, a place where women didn't just build businesses; they built each other. It's a place where they cried, created, and challenged one another to grow. Where they discovered strength in surrender, clarity in chaos, and connection in the spaces they least expected.

They call themselves BOOSTIES, and this year, we celebrate ten years of this bold, beautiful, purpose-filled community.

To honor this milestone, ten incredible BOOSTIES stepped forward to share their journeys. Their stories are tender, brave, and unfiltered, filled with joy and pain, grief and grace, breakdowns and breakthroughs. They are living proof of what happens when women rise because they chose to say "yes" to the BOOST.

And in doing so, they transformed pain into purpose, struggle into strength, and hope into action.

To celebrate this milestone, I want to introduce you to ten extraordinary women I'm honored to call BOOSTIES.

Betsy's faith is fierce. After unimaginable loss, she chose to turn heartbreak into hope and built a mission that helps others move from pain to purpose.

Gilza carries both wisdom and tenderness. As a therapist and truth-teller, she reminds us that the quiet nudges we feel are often the most powerful guides.

Maitte is grace under fire. A three-time cancer survivor, spiritual warrior, and radiant truth-teller, she shows us that real healing begins within.

Eva leads with heart. In the middle of life's messiness, she shows us that love and legacy walk hand in hand when you're caring for multiple generations at once.

Introduction

Luly found a different kind of strength in grief. After losing her husband, she discovered the unexpected power of community and a purpose in helping women rebuild from the inside out.

Barbie is fire. When life knocked her down, she didn't just rise, she lit the path for others. Her story is an invitation to come back to yourself, louder and brighter than ever before.

Daniela embodies healing. She shows us what it looks like to walk through fire and emerge softer, wiser, and ready to serve from a place of deep truth.

Mei takes us into the quiet shift that happens when a woman decides she matters again. Her journey reminds us that rediscovery can begin with something as simple as what's hanging in your closet.

Shannon traded safe for soul-stirring. Her story is a breathtaking reminder that honoring your roots can also mean giving yourself permission to fly.

Caro went from practicing law to practicing presence. She teaches us how to create a legacy and make an impact, at our own pace.

For more than a decade, I've watched hundreds of women rise through the BOOST community: women who dared to show up, speak their truth, own their power, and, yes, ask for a BOOST. These ten stories represent them. They're a reflection of what happens when we say yes— yes to giving a BOOST, yes to receiving a BOOST, and yes to being the BOOST.

Each woman here is living proof of what becomes possible when we stop pretending everything is fine and allow ourselves to receive. Together, they have given and accepted support through every season—with courage, with vulnerability, and with so much heart.

Now they're offering one to you. As you read, I invite you to reflect these questions on your own: Where in your life could you use a BOOST? Where are you being called to be the BOOST for someone else?

Generosity opens the heart. So does receiving. When we let others support us, we give them the gift of loving, serving, and holding space. Receiving isn't taking; it's honoring connection. Accepting a BOOST is saying yes to love in its most generous form. If we want to give fully, we must learn to receive fully. Inhale before you exhale. Fill up before you pour out.

So, take a breath. I pray these pages stir something deep inside you. That they feel like a breath of permission. That they remind you that rising was never meant to be a solo journey.

Remember the little girl who wasn't afraid to ask for help, who knew the incredible power that lives in community. Let this book remind you that you were never meant to climb alone. May it awaken that instinctive courage in you, and may you embrace the quiet grace of receiving.

So, let's begin. Because there's a BOOST waiting just for YOU.

Chapter 1

WHEN GOD CALLS YOU FOR MORE: HOW DARE YOU NOT LIVE YOUR PURPOSE TODAY?

BY BETSY GUERRA, PHD

Are you truly living your purpose?

If you don't know the peace that surpasses all understanding, the joy that transcends external circumstances, and the deep fulfillment that comes with readiness to "go" if God were to call you home today, then perhaps you aren't living your purpose.

To live your purpose is to rise into your highest self, in service of others with the gifts God placed in you. Purpose isn't what you do for a career, or the roles you play as a mother, wife, daughter, friend, or volunteer. Those may change, but your true purpose runs deeper. It's the sacred meeting place between your gifts and your passions, where your life becomes an answer to the needs of humanity. In that space, God's will for you takes shape, not as duty, but as desire. And in fulfilling it, you not only experience deep joy, but glorify Him in the process.

Purpose is not what you do. It's who you are.

With each season of life, roles change, experiences mold you, and identities evolve. But your essence, the truth of who you are, never changes. Your purpose is that which is constant. It's not the identity you adopted as a "mom" or "teacher" or "wife." It is the eternal thread God wove into you, unbroken since you were first imagined in His heart, carried in your mother's womb, and breathed into this world, all the way to the present moment.

When I was a little girl, I thought my purpose was to be a nun.

That changed really quickly the day I met my first boyfriend in seventh grade. Suddenly, the hopeless romantic inside me awoke, and with it, the longing to be swept off my feet by a knight in shining armor.

And I dreamt of the whole package of LOVE! The one that starts with the butterflies in your tummy, the Disney-style fireworks that light up your heart, and runs deep through your veins to reach the wrinkly hands that will be held in old age at your bedside.

I didn't know that love in real life, except in my dreams. Yet I desired it with all my heart. And desire, I would later learn, is often the whisper of purpose.

So, I began to wonder, was I born to be a wife?

Assuming that being a wife was my true purpose, I chased it with the strength and superpower of my faith. Faith has always been the core of who I am. Believing in what I cannot see (yet) comes naturally to me. I knew deep down that the person you choose to spend the rest of your life with is the most important decision you'll ever make, so I pursued it with intention.

I started with the inner work, guided by a therapist I began seeing while finishing my doctorate in psychology. That process led me to end a six-year relationship with my boyfriend. I loved him deeply, but I knew he wasn't the man God had prepared for me. He was such a good man, but not "perfect." At the time, I didn't know what "perfect" would look like, but I trusted that the right man would be someone whose flaws I could accept and even embrace for a lifetime.

Letting go of my boyfriend broke me. I cried myself to sleep night after night. And yet, in the middle of that pain, something life-changing happened.

I prayed.

But this prayer was different. One night, I opened my computer and poured out my heart in a letter to God.

Hi Papa Dios. I love you. I praise you. Thank you for being here with me caressing my hair as I lay on your lap and cry. I am so sad, Lord. I know you know. God, I feel compelled to pray for my husband. You've said, "ask and thou shalt receive," so here I am, Lord–asking. I would love for you to send me my prince as soon as I'm ready to receive him and embrace his love. Prepare me for him. Here's a list of everything I'd love in him, so you can prepare him too…

Below that short prayer was a list of "only" 130 things I wanted in my man. Yes, I was very specific. I knew what I wanted, from the deep stuff, like him being a man of faith and family, to the smaller things, such as him not peeing on the toilet seat.

Every time I noticed an amazing and loving quality in a man, I added it to my list. You can imagine that, with so many restrictions, no one I met made the cut. Some people joked that I'd stay a "jamona" (a spinster in Puerto Rican) with how picky I was, but I didn't mind. Although Mel Robbins wasn't yet famous to tell me so, I "let them," and I just kept praying for my man.

My faith in what I wanted never wavered. In fact, it grew into something deeper. I'd picture my husband and rejoice in our "future memories." I thanked God daily for him: *Thank you, Lord, for my husband. He's so amazing! Thank you for preparing him for me. He's perfect for me. I love him so much already!*

Less than two months later, I went to Brazil, and had a layover in Miami on the way back. In that Magic City, magic happened. My cousin introduced me to Alain, the man I instantly recognized as my beloved husband and the father of my children.

When God Calls You for More:
How Dare You Not Live Your Purpose Today?

Notice I didn't say I met him. I recognized him. It was a "there you are" kind of feeling. I had known and loved him all along. I couldn't see him before, but deep down I knew he existed, and I trusted that God would place him in my path at the right time. My faith revealed him to me. And when he finally stood in front of me, it was as if peace and joy came with the certainty of doing life with him.

That's what it feels like when you're living in alignment with your purpose.

While peace and joy abound in my heart with the decision of choosing Alain as my forever person, I still felt poked by "What's next? I want more."

"It must be that my purpose is to be a wife *and* a mom," I thought.

God, in His goodness, blessed us with Chichi, Fofi, Gordi, and Mia. I know their names sound like puppies, but no, they're actually our human kids. Each one came into our lives as pure love wrapped in tiny bodies that created an explosion of joy and a fulfillment I had never felt before. My heart overflowed.

At last I was *really* living my purpose!

Until…

August 25, 2013.

That morning, my almost three-year-old daughter, Fofi, pulled gently at my shorts while I was in the kitchen, getting everything ready for our family pool party.

"Mami, yo quiero estar donde tú estés," ("Mommy, I want to be where you're at,") she said with the cutest smile, making her request irresistible. What she really wanted was for me to be where she wanted to be… in the pool!

So I stopped everything I was doing and followed her. Soon after, Alain and our oldest, Chichi, joined us for our favorite cheerleading game. My one-year-old son was still napping, and Mia wasn't yet born. I carried the girls, one perched on each shoulder, while Alain lifted me up high. Together we formed our little pyramid, tiny hands raised in the air, laughter echoing across the water.

Those were the moments when joy was simple. When love was loud, playful, and overflowing. When everything felt complete.

Our friends and their kids started arriving. Chichi and Fofi ran to the edge of the pool to play with the other kids and the water toys. Everyone was having a great time, including the grandparents watching from the window, the guys at the tiki hut barbecuing, my friends splashing in and around the pool.

I was talking to a friend in the water when she suddenly asked, "Where's Fofi?"

The question hit me like a punch, triggering my nervous system. My heart leapt and my chest went tight. I scanned the pool, frantic though I had no reason to be. I couldn't see her. Where is Fofi? Where is Fofi? Then I looked right beside me—and there she was.

But at the bottom of the pool.

When God Calls You for More:
How Dare You Not Live Your Purpose Today?

I dove in, pulled her to my chest, and fought gravity to get her to the edge of the pool. She had a pulse. My friend, who's a doctor, began attending to her while someone called for an ambulance. I stepped back into a corner and tapped into my superpower. I prayed.

"Lord, please save her. You know I'm raising her for you, God. Please save her. Please!" Save her, Lord! Pleeeeaaaase save her!

We arrived at the hospital, and as my daughter lay lifeless on the stretcher, I kept begging God for mercy. The doctors were working on her, when my eyes suddenly drifted to a monitor with two lines. One moved in jagged zigzags. The other was straight and still. My heart stopped. Was that… a flat line?

Desperate, I pleaded, "Make her heart beat, Lord. Please make her heart beat. Make her heart beeeeaaaaat, God. Pleeeease make her heart beat!"

But He didn't.

God did not make my daughter's heart beat.

And with her last breath, the life I knew ended too.

Dark thoughts flooded my mind. My purpose was to be a mom, and a mom's main job is to keep their children alive. I failed. I can never live my purpose.

I believed I could never be happy again. That is… until someone I trusted told me otherwise.

My husband and I were hiding in the walk-in closet of our bedroom, trying to escape the crowd of friends and family filling the house. The priest who had baptized our children came and joined us in that small, quiet space.

Sitting on the floor in front of us, Alain asked with fear, "Father, you've seen this before. Is it possible to be happy again?"

The priest's reply was firm. "Some people are, and some people are never happy again."

Alain pressed on. "What makes the difference?"

"Those who are never happy again," he explained, "believe that their suffering proves their love. The more they cry, the more they think they're honoring their loved one. But those who find joy again understand that moving forward doesn't mean leaving behind. Love transcends death. They choose to honor their loved ones through love, service, and gratitude."

That was it. My purpose was to honor Fofi.

At the time, I had just begun my career as a professional speaker. I was invited to speak at a school. I prepared a polished psychology talk packed with clinical insights for the moms in the audience. But then, without planning to, I shared Fofi's story.

The room fell silent. Every eye turned to me. The mothers leaned in, captivated, completely immersed in my words.

And then fear gripped me. What am I doing? How can I hold their attention at her expense? How dare I use Fofi this way? In panic, I cut the story short and rushed back to my professional "safe" content.

Afterward, my dear friend and speaking coach, Caroline de Posada (Caro), pulled me aside. She looked at me, confused. "Why did you do that? You had them. Why did you change the subject?"

I told her my fear: that sharing Fofi's story meant I was benefiting financially from her loss and I couldn't allow that.

She shook her head gently. "You're not monetizing Fofi, Betsy. You're connecting with people. You're honoring her."

But I wasn't ready to believe that yet. I pushed back. Caro recognized I wasn't ready, and she let it go with grace.

While I wasn't willing to "monetize Fofi" in my talks, I was eager to grow my speaking business. My friend recommended a renowned coach.

February 8, 2017

I walked into the business coach's house not really sure what she could do for me, but trusting something good would come from it. People said this Luly B was a Miami celebrity, and I was curious to see what the buzz was about.

"Betsy, how did you do last year, and what's your vision for this one?" she asked when it was my turn to mastermind.

I laughed at myself, a little ashamed. "Well, I made a whopping $20k last year."

She didn't smile. "What else did you do last year?"

"Well, I was remodeling my house in the Keys, so I was the GC commuting three hours a day to haul materials and supervise the project."

"What else?" Luly asked, still serious, pen moving across her notepad.

"I dropped off and picked up the kids from school, cooked, drove them to their extracurriculars, helped with homework, kept up with the house and laundry, managed appointments…" I kept going as she kept asking, "What else?"

When I finally stopped, she looked down at her notes and read:

General Contractor — $50k

Babysitter — $50k

Housekeeper — $15k

Tutor — $5k

Driver — $12k

Therapist — $20k

"Betsy, if you had to pay for everything you did, you'd realize you were a six-figure producer last year. Don't ever talk about yourself that way."

Sigh.

Wow. She saw me. She named what had been invisible to me.

Because she believed in me, I believed, too.

In that moment, I stepped into the six-figure version of myself with intention. Over the next ten months, I grew my income from $20k to $120k while still carrying all those other roles.

What changed?

When God Calls You for More:
How Dare You Not Live Your Purpose Today?

Expansion. Luly and her Boost community lifted my mindset, belief, self-worth, support, and hope. They sparked my creativity and opened me to limitless possibilities.

One self-imposed limit I let go of was keeping Fofi out of my work. Compartmentalizing wasn't just draining; it violated the promise I made to myself the day I welcomed the priest into my walk-in closet: I will honor her through love, service, and gratitude.

"How dare I use Fofi to make money?" I asked one day at Luly's mastermind.

Her answer changed my life: **"How dare you NOT?"**

How dare you not share your story of Fofi to honor her? **How dare you not** offer hope to those standing where you once stood? **How dare you not** include the part of you that made you who you are today? **How dare you not**, Betsy?

The seed Caro planted was ready to sprout. A few weeks later, I gave my first speech that included Fofi. The standing ovation and the faces of awe in the audience matched the explosion of joy in my heart.

I was finally living my purpose.

My purpose is to be holy and whole, as my Heavenly Father created me. To fully use my God-given gifts in service to others. To live the dreams God dreams for me while lifting you. My purpose is... my pain transformed.

When I lost Fofi, I learned that all the wisdom from my doctorate in psychology wasn't enough. There were dark days when I thought I might lose my mind. But faith brought light to each moment and helped me move forward, little by little. Faith let me taste joy even when grief reigned. I had to share this with the world. That's when my psychotherapy practice, Better with Betsy, grew into a psycho-spiritual ministry.

It also gave birth to the Faith-Based Coaching Academy where I train and certify service-driven, heart-centered, faith-filled people as life coaches. In this internationally accredited program, I offer PhD-level training in psychology, guide them to connect with the indwelling God (the Holy Spirit), and teach them to weave this wisdom into daily life so they become living testimonies of love, peace, and joy.

Do you see it? Losing Fofi was the most excruciating pain of my life. But that loss became my greatest blessing. Not having her physically here to wrap her little hands around my neck in an embrace, taught me to love without seeing. It also led me to my greatness, my mission, and to a full heart. How can your pain become your purpose?

You and I were created for greatness. In our limited human minds, greatness often looks very different from the infinite greatness our Creator sees. My grief journey led me to an unwavering faith and a hope that shines so bright in my heart, that it's contagious and healing to others. My loss brought me face to face with the God of love and compassion who would embrace me and soothe my aching heart when the pain was unbearable. With Him, I came to truly know the peace that surpasses understanding and the steady joy that doesn't depend on outside circumstances.

The secret?

There are three.

The first one is—without a shadow of a doubt—FAITH. Faith is believing in what you cannot yet see, and acting as if it were already true so you may experience hope while you create that reality. Faith isn't only for the religious. You can have faith in yourself and in your ability to do hard things. You may also believe in others, have faith in the process, and trust in a higher power—who I call God. F.A.I.T.H. is also an acronym that describes practical psycho-spiritual tools that help you rise to your greatness. You may find these in my previous book: Hurt 2 Hope: Heal the pain of loss, grief, and adversity.

My dear friend Mindy once said, "My faith gave me faith." Faith is the gift that keeps on giving. It is the hope that helps you get up one more time, then one more time… because you see and believe in what is yet to manifest in your physical life.

The second secret is awareness; mastering self-understanding. My doctorate in clinical psychology and decades of experience gave me practical tools to rise again. I could've stayed bitter and depressed. I could've ended up in divorce and neglected my surviving children. I could have believed the lie that I would never be happy again. But psychology, powered by faith, helped me rise again. The same can be true for you.

The third key is community. You need people to help glue faith and awareness together. Community is the container God uses to bless and lift you. People can harm or heal; you get to choose those who elevate you and help pave your path to purpose. My family, therapist, hubby, children, priest, friends, clients, students, coaches, Caro, and Luly are highlights in my community.

Let me be part of yours.

So, what was my purpose, after all? The same as yours:

To be. To love. To shine bright and glorify God while I'm at it.

Depending on the season of life, my purpose looked differently: mom, wife, therapist, coach, teacher, friend, woman of faith. Your purpose is not attached to a role or identity, so you may live it no matter the season.

If you are single, love yourself with intention and grace. If you're married, live it as a devoted spouse. If your kids are little and require much of your time, live it in motherhood. If you stay at home, be the best housekeeper. If you're a professional, bring purpose to the people you serve. If your children are adults, be their best coach (and consider joining the Faith-Based Coaching Academy to deepen your confidence and connection with them).

Listen to the nudges within, the "I want more," and the "something's missing."

Permission granted to be grateful and still want more.

Be your purpose.

How dare you NOT?

About the Author

Dr. Betsy Guerra is a renowned psychotherapist, international speaker, coach trainer, and bestselling author who blends psychology and spirituality to help people rise above adversity and live with purpose. With over two decades of clinical and leadership experience, she has guided thousands of individuals and organizations to heal, grow, and thrive by embracing faith as a catalyst for transformation.

Betsy is the founder of Better with Betsy, the Faith-Based Coaching Academy, and La Fofi's Rainbow Foundation. Her work has been featured on NBC6, FOX11 Los Angeles, Univision, and the Las Vegas Morning Blend, as well as on leading podcasts and global stages. She is a member of the National Speakers

Association and has spoken at prominent events, including the Women Who Lead Summit, NSA Youth Leadership Program, William Grant and Sons, Legatus, and other major institutions like Florida International University, Miami-Dade Schools, and the University of Miami.

A trilingual leader fluent in English, Spanish, and Portuguese, Betsy is recognized, not only for her professional expertise, but also for her gift of weaving hope, joy, and resilience into every message she shares. Whether through her Faith & Growth Podcast, bestselling book Hurt 2 Hope, or her training of future coaches worldwide, Betsy inspires audiences to embody their God-given potential, transform challenges into opportunities, and live courageously in alignment with their true purpose.

You can reach Betsy directly at betsy@betterwithbetsy.com and experience her for free at GiftsFromBetsy.com

Chapter 2

FROM STUCK TO STARTING: RE-DISCOVERING YOUR VOICE IN BUSINESS

BY GILZA FORT MARTINEZ, LMFT

"Desire sparks a vision, but it's community that gives it life. Every time fear whispered, "Not yet," the voices around me said, "We'll go with you."

Those voices—mentors, peers, and friends, became my safety net. But the first spark always came from a whisper. That quiet, persistent feeling deep in your chest, nudging you toward something bigger, something you can't fully grasp yet. It's a whisper because the fear of failure, rejection, of feeling too young or too old can be overwhelming.

It's easy to ignore. It's easy to push aside. But it's powerful. And it deserves to be heard. If you've ever heard that whisper, try writing it down. Naming it is the first step in honoring it.

In my 30 years of working with women and their families, I've seen how many carry a quiet ache. They've done all the "right" things—built careers, earned degrees, supported families. From the outside, everything looks fine. But inside, there's a whisper: *"There's more for me... I want something different... I'm meant for more, but I don't know how and where to start."*

I know that whisper. I've heard it in my own life. I've felt its tug; soft at first, until it grew too strong to ignore, until it became louder than the fear holding me back. I've learned that the *whisper* is the first sign that you're ready to begin, even if you don't yet know the full path.

In my culture, stability is prized and risk is questioned, especially when you're a daughter. Even more so when you're the daughter of refugees. Leaving a salaried job to start my own psychotherapy practice felt like breaking an unspoken rule. Building Resolution Counseling Center on my own was an even bigger leap. It wasn't just against social expectations; it was against the version of myself that had been taught to play it safe.

But when I first heard that quiet voice whispering, *"try this,"* everything changed. Being in a community made that leap less terrifying. It transformed what could have felt like rebellion into a process of becoming.

DESIRE OVER FEAR.

That's the lesson I learned the first time I had to choose my voice: in college, and later in graduate school, when I chose psychology over law. Disappointing my parents was one of my biggest fears. I was supposed to be a lawyer, follow my father's path, continue his dreams, and keep the legacy of our family intact. For a while, I tried. I majored in Pre-Law, worked as a legal secretary and paralegal, and tried to suppress the pull of my true calling.

I was a junior in college when I first told my dad I wanted to do counseling. I'll never forget the look on his face. He said, "You want to work with crazy people?!" He laughed, but I could feel the seriousness beneath it. We both wanted to help people, just in different ways. He wanted to guide them through the law, while I wanted to guide them through the messy, beautiful complexity of human relationships. I was the "apple of his eye," so I tried to be what he wanted me to be.

I'm the child of political refugees from Cuba. My parents lost everything when they fled to find freedom. Security became everything, especially the kind that came with a steady paycheck. My father, an entrepreneur at heart, had learned through that immense loss to value stability above all else. He became a lawyer again while holding down a full-time job as a law librarian. That steady income acted as his safety net, and it gave him the freedom to follow his true passion: criminal defense law.

I understood his need for caution, but that caution made my own choices feel much heavier. It felt like every step I took might risk not only my own path but the dreams we all shared.

Fear doesn't always roar. Sometimes it whispers in logic: *"It's not the right time."* Sometimes it talks in guilt: *"Shouldn't I be grateful for what I have?"* Other times, it hides in self-doubt: *"What if I fail? Or worse, what if I succeed and can't keep it up?"* But along with fear, there's always another whisper—a quieter, more persistent one—that calls you toward your true self. It's the voice of desire, the voice of your inner soul, urging you to see what matters most and to notice what calls to you, even if it doesn't feel safe yet.

Listening to that whisper, and not letting fear control the narrative, was the first real act of reclaiming my voice.

Here's a quick tip on how to tell the difference between fear and desire: Pay attention to the direction of your energy. Fear makes you want to shrink back, to hide, while desire makes you curious, pushing you to lean in, even if your knees are shaking. The next time you're faced with a choice, notice whether you're trying to shrink back or if you're stretching forward. Add this answer to your writing. Let's start to keep track!

I took my first professional risk when I joined a rehab hospital, working with patients in pain. It was a place where collaboration was key. Every treatment plan was a team effort, and being a part of that team gave me a new kind of confidence. That first community became the space where I could hear the whisper of my true calling more clearly. Leaning into it made me believe in myself, not just as a counselor, but my confidence in my Self.

Next, I moved to a community mental health agency to finish my clinical hours for licensure. This wasn't about money, it was about service, devotion, and compassion. My dad was constantly worried, always reminding me to save, to prepare for what was ahead. Sometimes it felt like he was ridiculing my choices, or putting pressure on me.

But deep down, I knew it came from love. It gave me the psychological safety to take a risk, without losing my grounding, or my family.

Those early communities taught me a powerful lesson: meaningful growth doesn't happen in isolation. It happens in connection with others who challenge you, who see you, and who believe in you.

Who's in your corner, cheering you on and lifting you up?

DESIRE AND FEAR ARE OFTEN IN A TUG-OF-WAR INSIDE US.

And most of the time, they coexist. I know you've felt it too, even before reading this book. One of the biggest lessons I've learned is how to tell which voice is really calling the shots in my life. Fear is loud. It disguises itself as logic, obligation, or necessity. It can feel like a need to be practical, to play it safe. But desire is quieter. It comes in whispers; curiosity, energy, maybe even a little envy when you see someone else doing what you've been longing to do.

Desire pushes you forward, even when the path is unclear. It might not be as loud as fear, but it's persistent. The key isn't to eliminate fear, but to recognize that it doesn't have to control your decisions.

The second time I truly leaned into my own voice and followed my dreams fully was when I left the safety of the agency to start my own private practice. Security was behind me, and the unknown lay ahead. Fear was louder this time, but my desire was louder still. When I finally said it out loud—*I'm going to start my own practice*—I was hit with a wave of warnings. My parents, friends, even colleagues, all told me it was too risky. That I could lose everything I had worked for. Their fear fed mine. My mind became a storm: *What if they're right? What if I fail? What if I'm not as good as I think I am?*

Some even said I would "die of hunger." That it would be too hard to build and maintain a private practice. But beneath that storm, I could hear a quiet truth growing stronger: *I want to build something that's mine. Something that reflects not just what I can do, but who I am. I want to serve in a way that aligns with me, not who others think I should be.*

So, I listened again—this time to the quiet whispers of hope that said, "You don't have to do this alone."

An opportunity came to collaborate with two seasoned clinicians, who offered mentorship, referrals, and their business knowledge. It was a small community—just five of us, including me—but it became essential for my growth. It was there that my professional and entrepreneurial identity began to take shape.

If you're struggling with doubts, I encourage you to lean into the belief of at least one person who supports you. Let their belief carry you until your own faith in yourself grows. Keep walking the walk, until you can talk the talk!

As therapists, we study theories, the tools, the methods for helping and treating others. But no one teaches you how to start, run, or grow a business. And yet, private practice is a business, not just a calling. It demands systems, infrastructure, and strategy.

The mentors who came into my life were the ones who taught me to trust my inner voice, not as a critic, but as a compass. They became a part of my "Mirrors, Maps, and Motivators" framework. It's the same framework I now share with other women as they navigate their own dreams, creating paths that blend what they know with what they yearn to share with others.

The Mirror serves as a reflection of who you really are, beyond the doubts and labels. The Map reveals the steps ahead, even when the path isn't clear. And the Motivator reminds you why you started in the first place when fear sneaks back in.

I use this framework both symbolically and practically. This is where you return to your notebook, the one where you've been scribbling your whispers, your fears, your desires. The pages are more than just paper. They're a record of your journey, a map of what matters.

With your notebook in hand, I encourage you to truly "look in the mirror." Ask yourself the hard questions: What do I want? What's calling me? Where do I see myself in one, three, and five years?

I encourage you to lean into those whispers. This is a tool I've used in my own life. Every time a whisper would call to me, *I paused. I listened. I wrote it down.* Seeing it in black and white made a world of difference, not just for me, but for many of my clients too. It's helped them not only hear their whispers but start to follow them, step by brave step.

Writing helps create a "Map." Where do you want to start? What are the concrete steps? What might block your path? And once you know the terrain, I encourage you to build your tribe, people who will lift you up when you falter, people who will help you find your way when you're lost. Your tribe becomes your Motivator, the ones you turn to when doubts arise.

It's a slow process. It's full of moments of self-doubt, and sometimes, doubt from others. Creating my own unique Map helped me stay grounded, to believe in myself, even when it was hard. I've returned to that original Map over the years, honoring the fear, yes, but also my courage to keep moving forward.

Many women I work with today believe their voice is lost. But it isn't. It's just buried—under years of people-pleasing, endless responsibility, and choosing safety over self-expression. Reclaiming your voice starts small, with a whisper: *"I want more... I think I'm ready to try."* Growth doesn't begin with certainty. It begins with honesty—the courage to sit with uncertainty, to ask the hard questions, and to honor your fear.

For me, mentors were part of this journey, but the whispers were my compass—a subtle, steady guide. Listening to them taught me something powerful: community doesn't replace your inner voice; it amplifies it. And those whispers? They nudged me to trust myself, to take risks, to step forward even when fear loomed.

My mentors were invaluable, yet over time, one moved in a different direction. In 1998, I went out on my own. I started Resolution Counseling Center (RCC). And fear returned—along with guilt. Guilt is strange. It sneaks in quietly, colors your thinking, and questions your worth. *"Am I being disloyal? Shouldn't I be grateful for all I've done already?"* Practical doubts appeared too—finances, logistics, clients. Fear, doubt, and guilt intertwined, yet the whispers reminded me why I had started and what truly mattered.

During this time, I leaned on tools to stay grounded: journaling, list-making, weighing pros and cons. They helped me trust my intuition. *Don't be afraid to journal. It's not a test, and there's no right way. It's a chance to explore your thoughts, to hear those whispers and truly listen. To ask yourself: "What would I do if I could do anything?"*

Other lessons I carried with me: see your dream vividly in all its glory; learn to manage your expectations, not only of yourself but, more importantly, of others; treat mistakes as invitations to grow; and surround yourself with people who are aligned with your values and vision. Community is not just about support; it's about strategic alignment. Not everyone will share your vision, and not everyone will be willing to put in the strenuous work it requires. The right people can truly make all the difference.

Starting RCC was exhilarating. I had brought my vision to life by creating an office space designed exactly as I once envisioned while in graduate school, down to the paint color on the walls. That's why I encourage others to visualize their dreams with detail and color. In your notebook, draw out your dream. When you see it clearly, you're already halfway there.

But soon, life threw me into the unexpected. The mentor who had left his own practice to join me at RCC died suddenly. I was stunned. Though RCC was mine, I had counted on his wisdom, trusting that his guidance would help us grow. His death left me shaken, threw me off for some time. At the same time, I had just welcomed my second child, and his presence had given me the courage to return to work, not only for my clients but also for the future of RCC. Suddenly, that security was gone.

Then came more blows. Some team members left. One betrayed me. Fear returned, now carrying anger by its side. Anger often comes when we feel wronged or betrayed, and if we don't handle it properly, it can overwhelm us and create chaos. I realized I had to relearn old, simple lessons, like the ones we hear in kindergarten: "play well with others." Life has a way of reteaching us through fire, not comfort.

That betrayal forced me to grow in ways I didn't expect. I had to find my voice, but more importantly, I had to learn how to regulate it. Again, I leaned into the whispers saying, *"Stay true. Don't let this compromise your values."*

I had always believed that loyalty and generosity would lead to success. But one of the hardest lessons I learned was that befriending business colleagues, especially when their values didn't align with mine, could leave me vulnerable.

Looking back, I can see how I set myself up for disappointment, but in the moment, it was painful, confusing, and shocking.

What helped me heal was learning to set boundaries. Boundaries are not walls. They don't shut people out. Instead, they guide us, protecting our energy and our peace.

So, I'll ask you what I had to ask myself then: *Where in your own life can you set a loving but firm boundary, so you can clear space to hear the whispers meant for you?*

None of us are meant to do this alone, whatever "this" is for you. I often see women isolate themselves, waiting for confidence, clarity, or the perfect moment, afraid to speak their dreams out loud. I learned that **confidence grows in community.** So, I regrouped and focused on people who shared my vision. My practice, RCC, steadied. I was finally building my own roadmap.

I had reached my original dream: independence, money, and sharing resources; and yet restlessness returned. Though I shared space with other therapists, we were separate. That created a sense of community but not a real connection. After years of quiet stability at RCC, I listened to the whispers again. They reminded me to honor my voice and my purpose. In 2019 I hired a young, woman-owned marketing firm and brought in new systems: digital calendars and a branded website. These weren't new ideas to the world, but they were new to me. Fear came back; money, exposure, vulnerability. But this new community guided me, held my hand, and amplified those whispers.

I stayed open to learning and to how others were developing and evolving. I met Luly B. Carreras and joined her community called BOOST, and it named what had always been calling me but that I couldn't name. *Here, I learned the power of collaboration over competition.* Vulnerability became another tool. It helped me rethink my vision and reset my goals. Long-ignored dreams like writing, speaking, making a broader impact, all came back into view. Listening to those whispers, leaning into her community, and trusting their support gave me courage, confidence, and connection. Soft whispers grew louder. My next roadmap was clarity. *It's never too late to dream again.*

Starting something from the ground up—whether it's a business, a career, or a whole new chapter of life—feels impossible at times. The walls feel so high, the motivation so low, and the inner critic? It never shuts up. But *connection*, that's what pulls you through. When you're surrounded by women who get it, who have felt the same fear and doubt, you stop questioning yourself. You start to borrow their belief in you. You find your way out of the stuck places quicker. And those whispers? They get louder, reminding you that your voice was always here, just waiting for you to hear it.

> *It always seems impossible until it's done.*
>
> **– Nelson Mandela**

If you've been waiting for permission, here it is. You don't have to be fearless. What you need is the courage to show up. Growth comes from being willing; willing to ask the tough questions (use your Mirror), willing to be honest, and willing to face the fear without letting it take control. Listen to the quiet whispers (create your Map), even when fear tries to drown them out. Your voice hasn't disappeared. It's just waiting for you to speak it. Trust yourself. Trust your voice. Let the right people (your Motivators) help carry you forward.

 Breathe. Believe.

About the Author

I'm Gilza Fort Martinez LMFT, wife, mom, and Marriage & Family Therapist with over 30 years of experience, and the founder of Resolution Counseling Center in Miami, FL. I first felt the pull between fear and desire when I chose to start my own practice, despite warnings from family, friends, and colleagues. In my chapter, I share how I struggled with expectations, especially from my parents, versus what was truly calling me. Since then, I've worked with hundreds of women, helping them learn to find, trust, and use their voices for themselves, their dreams, and their businesses.

I hope my story inspires you to listen to those quiet whispers of hope and trust yourself enough to explore new paths. Outside of work, I enjoy gardening with my husband and spending time with my grown daughters. You can follow my journey on Instagram **@Toughlovehealer**, Facebook and LinkedIn **Gilza Fort Martinez**, or visit **gilzafort.com** to connect and share your own story with me.

https://www.gilzafort.com/

Chapter 3

LET GO OF YOUR PAST, TRUST IN YOUR FUTURE

BY MAITTE PENALVER

You Have "Cancer"

I remember that moment as if it happened yesterday, I was sitting in that sterile doctor's office, waiting for words that I feared but somehow knew would come. Then, they came: "You have cancer." It wasn't just disbelief; it was like my entire world had fallen apart. At 41, a mother to a young child, I felt like everything I had worked for, all my dreams, just vanished in an instant. I wasn't the first woman, the first mother, or the first wife to have been diagnosed with this disease. But I was me, Maitte, and that made my experience one of a kind, no matter how many times those words had been spoken before.

The world turned cold, and I felt as though my dreams had disappeared right along with it.

You have "Cancer" Again

They say that hearing "You're in remission" should be like crossing the finish line of a long, grueling race. And don't get me wrong, there was relief, there was joy. But if I'm honest, there was also something else, something I didn't expect.

After the breast cancer, I thought I had beaten the race. I thought I had made it to the end. But just a few years later, cancer came knocking again. Non-Hodgkin's lymphoma. It arrived in the middle of a pandemic, when life already felt like it had been thrown into chaos. Imagine learning that your second cancer diagnosis came at a time when hospitals were more like war zones, nurses and doctors dressed in protective gear that made them look like scientists in a movie, and the world outside felt like a distant memory. On top of that, I was homeschooling my child, trying to work, and constantly faced with the terrifying uncertainty of not just cancer, but COVID. The doctors were clear: If I contracted COVID, I wouldn't survive — since I had no immune system left to fight. Yet, somehow, I survived

YOU SURVIVED. NOW WHAT?

Not once, but twice. And then, as if I hadn't been through enough, came the third cancer diagnosis. I remember laughing nervously, wiping away the tears. Was this some kind of sick joke? What kind of cruel twist was this? What I didn't know then was that the worst was yet to come; a stem cell transplant. That was the battle that nearly destroyed me.

It felt like my body had been torn apart and rebuilt from the ground up. I didn't even recognize myself anymore. My body, my mind, everything about me felt foreign. The healing process? It was something I could've never prepared for.

People called me a warrior. They said I was the strongest person they knew. They celebrated my wins, shared my photos, and wrote captions about courage and faith. And I appreciated every bit of it. But as the days passed, and the cards stopped coming, and the casseroles were no longer showing up at my door, I found myself sitting alone in my living room, with one question I didn't expect:

Now what?

Who am I now? What happened to my body, my mind, my life? Why do I feel so… lost?

I never rang the bell symbolizing the end of treatment because, with this third diagnosis, I didn't get the "remission reward" most people do.

It wasn't that I wasn't grateful. I was deeply, painfully so. I was alive. But I was also carrying a weight I wasn't prepared for: questions, fears, and a kind of emptiness that made me feel like I no longer fit in my own life anymore. The treatment drained me.

I was exhausted, immunocompromised, and unable to do anything that brought me joy for months. What should have been a time to celebrate felt like a time to dread. I spent 80 percent of my days alone. I couldn't drive, I couldn't eat, and I certainly couldn't live the life I was promised by the latest treatment. Despair became my closest companion.

And if you've ever felt this way after your own battle, hear me:

You're not broken.

You're not ungrateful.

You're not falling behind.

You're healing.

And healing, that's the most important part of this journey.

THE MYTH OF GOING BACK TO NORMAL

Here's the thing I wish more people would say out loud: there's no going back.

Before cancer, before the infusion rooms, before the bald head staring back at me in the mirror, before the isolation where the walls felt like they were closing in—there was a version of life I had. That version is gone. It's not coming back, no matter how hard you wish it could. Trying to squeeze yourself into it is like trying to fit into a pair of jeans you outgrew long ago. It's uncomfortable, painful, and unsustainable.

But still, the world around you will tell you that you can get back to normal.

"You beat it!" they'll say. "Everything will go back to the way it was."

But your body tells a different story. Scars, neuropathy, exhaustion that sneaks up on you after folding a load of laundry. Your spirit tells a different story too, long nights spent staring at the ceiling, wondering if every ache is "something."

The gap between who you were and who you are now? It's real. It's raw. And it feels like grief.

Because, in many ways, it is grief.

You are allowed to grieve the life you lost, while still being grateful for the life you have. These two emotions don't have to be at war with each other. They will sometimes clash, and other times, they will hold hands, walking side by side. But ultimately, they are companions, necessary ones in the journey.

MAKING PEACE WITH A PAINFUL PAST

Survivorship is often compared to returning from war, and I believe it. But my war didn't have soldiers or gunfire. It had hospital gowns, PICC lines, chest ports, endless surgeries, painful blood draws, and that sterile, antiseptic smell that clung to my skin and clothes long after I left the hospital.

My war had nights when my heart raced with the fear that my body might give up before the morning came. It had moments where I whispered desperate prayers for strength, while chemo burned through my veins and my bones ached as if they were being torn apart from the inside.

When you've lived through something like that, you can't just "move on." You can't pretend the battle didn't change you. You have to make peace with it. And making peace doesn't mean ignoring the hurt, it means standing face-to-face with it, looking it in the eye, and deciding: This shaped me, but it doesn't get to define me.

For me, making peace has looked like:

Forgiving my body for betraying me, for getting sick.

Allowing myself to feel the fear I buried so deep during treatment.

Releasing the guilt that I survived when others didn't.

Some days, making peace means looking at the scars in the mirror and saying, thank you for carrying me through.

RECONNECTING WITH THE SELF BENEATH THE "SURVIVOR"

The label "survivor" is meant to be empowering, and in many ways, it is. There are moments when I wear it with pride, grateful for the reminder of all I've overcome. It's a testament to my strength, to the battles I've fought, and to the resilience that helped me push through when I thought I couldn't.

But there are other times when it feels like a weight. It's as though the world sees only that one part of me, as if my entire identity is defined by the hardest thing I've lived through.

Yes, I am a survivor. But I am also a mother who laughs way too loud at my son's jokes. A friend who treasures long coffee dates that stretch for hours. A coach who finds joy in helping others dream bigger, and a woman who, even now, is still figuring out what happiness looks like. I am layered, and "survivor" is just one piece of my story, not the whole of it.

I often find myself asking: Who was I before cancer? Who am I becoming now?

The truth is, I had to give myself permission to be more than the woman who survived three cancers. I had to give myself the space to be me again, to find out what it meant to live fully in a life that had been shaken to its core. That permission meant trying new things without caring whether I was good at them. It meant letting go of relationships that drained me, even if they had been a part of my life for years. It meant saying yes to what truly ignited something in me—and no to the things that didn't feel right deep down.

I am so thankful for the communities of friends and groups that surrounded me during some of my darkest moments. Some days, reconnecting with myself was as simple as reading a book, buying flowers for my kitchen table, or finally signing up for the BOOST Community I'd been putting off for ages. Other days, it was about sitting quietly with myself and asking, "What do I really want?"

What I've learned is this: survivorship is not the finish line. It's not a neat ending where everything magically returns to "normal." Survivorship is a doorway, a wide-open invitation to create the next chapter of my life, on my terms.

You get to decide who you're becoming.

You get to rediscover parts of yourself that cancer never touched and uncover new pieces you never knew existed. Most importantly, you get to define yourself—not by what you survived, but by how you choose to live now.

WHEN THE WORLD THINKS YOU'RE "BETTER"

After my last treatment, it felt like everyone around me let out a collective sigh of relief, as if we'd all crossed the finish line. Friends and family celebrated, congratulated me, and said, "You must be so happy it's all behind you." They meant well, and part of me wanted to believe them. But deep down, I knew that wasn't the truth. That's when the real work began.

The calls stopped coming. The meals stopped arriving. Life moved forward for everyone else, while I stood still, trying to put myself back together. To them, the cure was the end of the story. But for me, it was just the beginning of a new chapter, one I didn't fully understand yet.

I had to learn how to trust my body again, something I hadn't realized I'd lost until I tried to listen to it. Every ache or twinge brought a jolt of fear.

Fatigue and brain fog were my constant companions. And those follow-up appointments? They felt like emotional landmines, each one setting off a chain of "what ifs" I was trying so hard to avoid.

One of the biggest lessons I've learned since then is this:

I don't owe anyone a performance of resilience.

I don't have to be "inspiring" every day.

And I sure as hell don't need to wear a brave face when I'm struggling inside.

It's okay to say, "I'm not okay today."

It's okay to need space, rest, or even a good cry—for no reason other than the fact that your soul is exhausted. Healing isn't a straight line, and there's no deadline for it.

Not all wounds are visible. The scars we carry inside deserve the same care, patience, and compassion as the ones that can be seen. And sometimes, the most courageous thing you can do is admit you're still figuring it out. That's where true healing starts.

TOOLS TO REBUILD TRUST IN YOUR BODY, MIND, AND SOUL

Healing isn't a straight line. Some days, you'll feel solid and rooted. Other days, it might feel like you're sinking in quicksand. That's okay. It's part of the process.

These are the practices that have helped me find my way back to myself:

1. **Body Check-Ins** – Every morning, I ask myself: *What do I need today? Where am I holding tension? How can I show up for myself right now?*

2. **Gentle Movement** – It's not about getting my old body back. It's just a way to remind myself, *I'm still here*. A slow walk, some stretching—whatever feels right.

3. **Mindful Journaling** – My journal holds both my gratitude and my grief. Here are some prompts that help me:
    - Today I feel...
    - What I wish others understood is...
    - I'm proud of myself for...

4. **Digital Boundaries** – I've learned to curate my social media. I choose what I allow in, making sure it feeds my soul rather than drains it.

5. **Anchor Rituals** – Simple things like lighting a candle, making a cup of tea, taking five deep breaths, or walking outside. These small acts reassure my nervous system: *You're safe now*.

PERMISSION TO GRIEVE—AND TO CELEBRATE

There are days when I miss the hair I lost, the energy I once had, the carefree version of myself who didn't yet know how fragile life could be.

And yet, there are also days when I find myself celebrating the woman I've become; the resilience, the compassion, the way I can find beauty in even the smallest of moments.

It's okay to grieve and to celebrate at the same time. There's no contradiction in that.

SHIFTING SPIRIT AND MINDSET: FROM FEAR TO FAITH

When you're faced with the reality of your own mortality, fear can often feel like a constant companion. Every time I go in for a scan, I hold my breath, waiting for the ground to shift beneath me.

But over time, I've learned to let faith take the wheel instead of fear.

For me, faith isn't always religious, it's simply the belief that:

- My body can heal and be trusted again.
- My life holds meaning beyond just my diagnosis.
- It's safe to hope again.

Some days, faith is as simple as taking a deep breath, just being present in the moment. Other days, it's as if I'm holding my hands together, whispering to the heavens above. But on the hardest days, faith might just be the quiet whisper, *I am here. I am alive.*

You don't have to try to rebuild the life you had before cancer. You get the chance to create something new, something that aligns with who you are now.

Purpose doesn't have to be grand or flashy. It can be:
- Speaking kindly to yourself, even when it's hard.
- Supporting someone who's just starting their own journey.
- Saying *no* when you'd normally say *yes*.
- Allowing yourself to rest without the weight of guilt.

Your past is not your punishment. Your diagnosis does not define you. Healing is not a destination—it's the way you learn to become, little by little.

CLOSING INVITATION

You have walked through fire. You have carried what most people can't imagine. And still, you are here.

Let the woman you were rest. Thank her. Bless her. She brought you this far.

You are not starting over. You are starting again with more truth, more clarity, and more courage than before.

If you hear nothing else from me, hear this:

You are not broken.

You are becoming.

You are healing, and you are here.

"Hope" is the thing with feathers
That perches in the soul
And sings the tune without the words
And never stops at all.

—Emily Dickinson

About the Author

Hi, I'm Maitte Penalver. My journey through cancer has shaped me in ways I never imagined, and now I'm passionate about helping others heal the emotional and psychological wounds left by a cancer diagnosis.

With a background in English and a love for storytelling, I've always turned to writing and journaling as tools to process life's hardships. After battling cancer three times, including undergoing a stem cell transplant, I offer a unique firsthand perspective on the challenges cancer patients face—not just physically, but emotionally and spiritually.

In my chapter, I share a raw look at the often-hidden struggles of survivorship, offering insight into how you can heal and discover a life of deeper meaning. I've walked this path, and now I'm here to help you find your own. I hope that my story will inspire you to move forward with strength, purpose, and an open heart.

If you're navigating this journey, you're not alone. Let's explore how you can transform your experience into something powerful.

maitte@maittepenalver.com

Chapter 4

GUIDED BY FAITH – EMPOWERED TO PLAN

BY EVA GONZALEZ

How Faith, Community, and Proactive Planning Help Us Care for Parents, Raise Children, and Leave a Legacy of Love

Have you ever tried talking to your parents about their end-of-life plans? If you're anything like me, it probably didn't go as smoothly as you hoped. I remember trying to bring it up with my dad, and he became so upset. He looked at me sternly and asked, "Why are you trying to kill me?" That comment broke my heart. All I wanted was to ensure we knew his wishes, so when the time came, we could honor them. But it was hard to even start the conversation.

Now, picture this: you're juggling your own life, maybe a child or grandchild pulling at your sleeve, and then you get a call from your mom: "Papi's in the hospital. You need to fly to Puerto Rico right away!" That's been my reality. It's one of the toughest seasons of my life.

That's what they mean when they call us the "sandwich generation." The term refers to middle-aged adults who are simultaneously caring for aging parents and raising children. Some of us, like me, are even grandparents now. I've got seven grandkids so far, yeah seven to be exact! It's a lot, right? You might be in the thick of raising your children or helping them step into adulthood while, at the same time, taking care of your parents, keeping up with doctor's appointments, school events, financial worries, legal paperwork, career responsibilities, and the emotional weight of trying to do it all. I see you because I've been there too.

For me, the only way I've made it through these seasons of life has been by holding onto three anchors: Faith, Community, and Planning.

My Catholic faith has always been my foundation, a steady presence since childhood. Alongside that, my various communities: faith-based, women-focused, and business-related have boosted me through each stage of my journey. And a commitment to planning, especially in helping others to plan, has brought a sense of clarity and confidence to the chaos that often surrounds me.

This chapter is as much my story as it is a roadmap for you. I want to remind you: You are not alone. You don't have to carry this weight on your own. There is peace to be found, strength to be gained, through faith, through community, and through creating a plan that centers the people you love most.

MY FAITH COMMUNITY – THE FOUNDATION

From the very start, my Catholic faith has been my constant. I was blessed with a family that supported me: my parents, Manuel and Cuca; my brother, Manny; and my beautiful sister and best friend, Lyda. Growing up, attending Mass, going on retreats, and participating in various ministries played a pivotal role in shaping who I am today.

Groups like Experiencia Cristo, which I was part of in my youth, and later Camino, Cursillo, Emmaus, Impactos, and MOMS (Ministry of Mothers Sharing), all provided me with what I needed at different points in my life. Each community offered its own unique form of support, teaching me lessons, challenging my thinking, and filling me with the strength to keep moving forward.

Raising my eight children, I often relied on the communities that became my lifelines. For those of you thinking, *"How in the world did she manage with eight kids?"* (trust me, I get that a lot), my answer is simple: Christ in my life, a supportive and hands-on husband, Jorge, and, of course, a color-coded calendar.

I'm not joking. I had each kid on their own color codes, as well as our business and social events. Even the back-to-school shopping list lived in a spreadsheet.

But even with all that structure, life still felt heavy sometimes. That's when community came through, making all the difference. I'll never forget the day my "personal interior decorators" showed up. Jorge was always traveling, the kids kept me busy, and we'd just wrapped up construction on our home. Our artwork was still leaning against the walls, waiting for a "someday" that never came.

Then, one afternoon, four friends came over and, in a matter of hours, transformed our space. They didn't just hang up pictures, they decorated my heart. In that moment, I felt truly seen and loved.

That's what community does. It shows up when you need it the most, reminding you that you're never really alone.

Not every story is pretty or easy to tell. My mom, whom I love with all my heart, sure knew how to push my buttons. (She's mellowed in her older years and, by the way, knows I can't get pregnant anymore, LOL.) She never quite understood why Jorge and I had so many children, and would often ask, "Is this the last one?" Most of the time, I'd brush it off. But on one particular day, we were heading to the airport because she was returning to Puerto Rico, and she asked again, "Is this the last one? Please tell me you're not going to have another."

Mind you, I was pregnant with our fifth child, Ana, and that was the moment I snapped. My emotions were all over the place, and as we neared the Departures area, I lost my temper. I said some not so nice things, things I'm not proud of and, in a fit of frustration, told her to get out of the car. Not one of my finest moments, to say the least.

What sticks with me, though, is what happened next. After everything settled down, my friends showed up. They told me to meet them at the school parking lot before pickup. And there they were, waiting for me, ready to love me through my brokenness. That's what community looks like.

Then came the meal trains. After Ana was born, meals arrived at my door for weeks. The same thing happened after Lili (6 of 8), Tina (7 of 8), and Carlitos (8 of 8) were born. That outpouring of generosity stuck with me. Since then, I've made it a point to return the favor. Whenever someone in my circle has a baby or is facing a tough time, I show up with food. I'll never forget one friend, Mercy, who had been a recipient of a meal train. She asked me to always include her in future ones, so she could pay it forward. It's a perfect example of how love multiplies when we share it.

During the pandemic, we "adopted" an older gentleman from our parish. He was living in an assisted living facility and had very few visitors, so we made weekly trips to see him. My kids played games with him, listened to his stories, and learned that love doesn't have to be complicated. We can give our time, our talents, and our treasure to those who need it most, even if it's just by showing up. In doing so, we also taught our children how they can care for the elderly in our family. Remember, you're training them to care for you one day.

Through all these experiences, I've come to understand the power of surrounding myself with "balcony people." Years ago, I read Balcony People by Joyce Landorf Heatherley. In it, she talks about how some people bring you down; what she calls basement people, while others lift you up, those are your balcony people. I've been fortunate enough to find balcony people within my faith communities, and I've tried to be that person for others as well.

Scripture says it so beautifully in 1 Thessalonians 5:11: "Therefore encourage one another and build each other up, just as in fact you are doing."

That's exactly what balcony people do. They lift you, cheer you on, and remind you of your worth when you've lost sight of it. And at the same time, we are called to be that balcony person for someone else.

MY BOOST COMMUNITY – EMPOWERED BY WOMEN

If my faith community was the solid foundation that held me up, my BOOST community gave me wings to soar. It all began when my friend Betsy Guerra invited me to Spark. That day, I won a ticket to the Superwoman Retreat, where I met the amazing Luly B. That introduction opened the door to a whole new circle of women, go-getters, dreamers, and real-life cheerleaders. Honestly, Luly is truly *"a magnet for awesomeness!"*

From Café con Luly to planning workshops and even the small gatherings with my POD at Starbucks, every event left me feeling energized. Whether you're an introvert or an extrovert like me (I always joke with my kids that "strangers are just friends I haven't met yet"), we all long to be seen, heard, and supported. And when you find your tribe, those people who truly love you, challenge you, and want the best for you, you just know it. It's a feeling that can't be described, only experienced.

BOOST didn't just bless me personally; it lifted me professionally too. My husband and I have a real estate team, and thanks to my communities, we've seen incredible growth. For two years in a row, I've sponsored a table for ten women at Spark, inviting friends I knew would benefit from the event. Watching them light up, feeling the energy in that room, was such a gift. It reminded me of how Betsy did the same for me all those years ago, and I feel blessed to pay it forward.

BOOST also taught me something crucial: always put family first. At the workshops, we were encouraged to schedule vacations before business commitments. That shift gave me permission to prioritize what truly matters. Now, Jorge and I cherish our "Last-Friday-of-the-Month" beach dates and family vacations as non-negotiables. These moments help us recharge and refocus for everything else. We all need to take time for ourselves. Another lesson I picked up from my business community: if it's not in your calendar, it doesn't exist. So, make sure to schedule what's important!

MY BUSINESS COMMUNITIES – LIFELINES AND LAUNCHPADS

Speaking of business communities, the first one I joined was Pivot: Shift Ahead. It launched on March 16, 2020, the day the world shut down. Real estate coach James Shaw sent out a Zoom link, and a handful of us joined. We didn't know what the future would hold, but we knew we needed each other.

That call has kept going strong ever since. Realtors from across the U.S. and Canada log in daily to share tips, ask questions, and support one another. Pivot has become a staple in my routine, a constant reminder that I'm never alone.

On July 26, 2022, my father passed away. I felt lost, heartbroken, and unsure of what to do next. The grief was overwhelming. But then, friends who had walked that same path shared their own stories with me. In that moment, I realized I wasn't alone.

A month later, in August, I attended a Keller Williams event called **Mega Camp**. During the event, I heard Dan Ihara speak. Dan, from the Ihara Team with KW Realty Honolulu and founder of the KW RE Planner community, shared his work with the Keller Williams Real Estate Planner community. He explained how he helps people with strategic planning for life's major transitions, guiding families through senior relocations, trusts, probate, 1031 exchanges, and even divorce.

What he said struck a chord with me. As I listened, I thought to myself: *I want to do that too.*

I couldn't help but wish I had known about this sooner, before my dad passed. But as they say, when the student is ready, the teacher appears.

The KW Real Estate Planner community focuses on helping families plan proactively for those big, often complicated life changes. From senior relocations to navigating trusts, 1031 exchanges, probate, and divorce, it's sensitive work, but necessary. Through this community, I've gained the tools to serve families with compassion and confidence.

When life throws these curveballs, we can be that trusted advisor, guiding them through the next steps, especially when it comes to real estate. Is it time to sell, or should they hold on to the property? It's about helping them make decisions that will ease their journey, just as I wish someone could've helped my family during our hardest days.

In this community, I found my tribe once again, people who, like me, are passionate about helping families plan with love before a crisis forces their hand. Every week, we come together to brainstorm ways to make this happen. That shared mission and support fuel me to keep serving others, not only with their real estate needs but also by helping them create strategies that minimize, or even avoid, family disputes.

REMEMBER THE ROADMAP?

Enough about me, let's talk about you. If you're balancing the responsibility of caring for your parents while raising or launching kids, you already know how exhausting it can be. One moment, you're in the kitchen preparing dinner; the next, you're on the phone with your mom's doctor. You're rushing to drop one kid off at practice while still worrying about whether your dad took his medication. You're drowning in paperwork, bills, and appointments, all while trying to keep your marriage strong and your relationship exciting.

The guilt can feel overwhelming. You wonder if you're doing enough for your parents while fearing you're falling short with your kids. The emotional toll of caregiving is grueling, and it doesn't stop there. It can also lead to financial strain, as you try to manage the needs of both younger and older family members. I've worked with families who've had to sell their parent's home, or even their own, to cover the costs of care. Believe me, friends, I know how heavy this feels because I've been there.

But here's the truth I've learned: you can't do this alone. For me, it's these three anchors; faith, community, and planning, that make the load bearable.

Faith keeps you grounded when everything else feels like it's falling apart. My morning routine is non-negotiable time spent with God through scripture reading, prayer, and journaling. It's how I begin each day, centered and reminded that He is always with me. I often share with my prayer angels: God works through us every day, if we're paying attention. I remind myself to ask, "Who can I serve today?" and then simply say, "Jesus, I trust you."

Community gives you the BOOST you need when you feel like you can't carry the weight alone. This BOOST might be a friend who shows up with dinner, a women's group that surrounds you, or a mastermind that holds you accountable. But no matter what form this BOOST takes, find your tribe. You don't have to go through this journey alone.

Planning brings peace of mind. It doesn't eliminate the challenges, but it gives you clarity and confidence to face them, instead of feeling lost in crisis and confusion.

A TASTE OF PROACTIVE PLANNING

Planning doesn't have to be complicated. Some family members dive into planning with open arms, and it brings them peace. My in-laws are like that. For them, having everything in place means they won't be a burden to their six boys. It's a relief to know that the groundwork has been laid out in advance.

My mom, though, always wanted to be prepared. But, like many of us, she didn't really take action until my father passed away. After his funeral, she turned to me and said, "Let's get my things in order." God bless her. In those words, I could hear the peace it gave her, even in the midst of her grief.

Then, there are parents who refuse to have the conversation at all. They avoid talking about wills, end-of-life plans, or anything that could feel uncomfortable. If that sounds familiar, here's where you can start:

Start the conversations. Gentle, love-first talks are far better than the arguments that come later. Trust me, I've learned this the hard way—in cars, and even with my dad's "Are you trying to kill me?" comment when the subject of wills came up.

The key is to plan before the crisis hits. A little preparation now can save you mountains of stress later on.

Build your team. Think about the professionals you'll need: an estate planning attorney, a financial planner, an accountant, and yes, a real estate planner. It's never too early to have the right people by your side.

Show up for both generations. As you care for your parents, involve your kids when you can. It teaches them empathy and helps them understand the value of a legacy.

And always remember that you are not alone. God didn't design us to walk this path alone. Find your balcony people, the ones who lift you up, and be that person for someone else. We were made for community.

When you piece these things together, you're not just creating a plan. You're creating a legacy of love. And that's something beautiful.

Looking back, I can see how community has boosted me through every season: through my faith circles, my BOOST sisters, and my business masterminds. They've seen me, supported me, and walked alongside me. The greatest lesson I've learned from all of this is simple: focus on what you can control and let go of what you can't. Love your parents. Raise your kids. And most importantly, remember that you don't have to do it alone.

Planning with love is the greatest gift you can give your family. When you plan, you remove fear and confusion. You create peace. You leave behind a legacy of love, not loose ends. As 2 Timothy 1:7 reminds us: "For God has not given us a spirit of fear; but of power and of love and of a sound mind." And as Proverbs 3:5-6 says: "Trust in the Lord with all your heart and lean not on your own understanding; in all your ways acknowledge Him, and He shall direct your paths."

Friend, you are not alone. Guided by faith and empowered to plan, you can walk through this season with confidence, clarity, and love.

About the Author

Hi, I'm Eva Gonzalez—a proud mom of eight, grandmother of seven, and a woman whose life is deeply guided by faith, family, and community.

As an agent with Team Dad of Eight, powered by Keller Williams Premier Properties, I wear many hats, including Senior Real Estate Specialist (SRES) and Certified KW Real Estate Planner. With more than a decade of experience, I've dedicated my career to helping families build, protect, and transfer generational wealth through real estate. I have a special passion for serving seniors and the sandwich generation, supporting them through some of life's biggest transitions with care and understanding.

In my chapter, I share how community has been my anchor while caring for my parents and raising a big family. My journey has taught me that with faith, community, and proactive planning, we can honor our loved ones and create a legacy of love, not loose ends.

When I'm not serving families, you'll likely find me sailing with my husband, Jorge, planning our next travel adventure, soaking up a beach day, or making memories with our children and seven grandchildren.

My hope is that my story encourages you to lean on your faith, draw strength from your community, and plan your future with love and confidence. And if you don't yet have that support, I pray that God guides you toward the right people to walk with you on this journey.

Let's Connect:

- Email: eva@DadOf8RealEstate.com
- Instagram: @evamomof8
- LinkedIn: linkedin.com/in/eva-m-gonzalez

Chapter 5

WIDOWED BUT NOT BROKEN: A MOTHER'S JOURNEY TO COMMUNITY, STRENGTH, AND A NEW CALLING

BY LULY CORDOBA

December 21, 2022

"I'm not ready for you to go. But everyone keeps telling me I need to let you know it's okay if you need to. I'm not Mi Tesoro, but if you have to, then I'll let you go. I promise I won't be mad at you, but I will miss you and love you forever."

I kissed him, held his hand, laid my head on his chest, and fell asleep. His breathing had calmed a little, and as I drifted off, I felt a small sense of relief that he didn't seem to be struggling so much.

Three hours later, I woke up to our dog, Riley, barking. Riley had been sleeping under Douglas' hospital bed. It was at this moment the nurse walked in. She spoke softly, and what I thought I heard her say was, "He's breathing better." But when I looked at my husband, saw no movement, and touched his chest, then I knew I heard her wrong. With my heart already in my throat, I looked at her, and looked at my husband and said, "He's not breathing at all."

Her gaze softened with compassion, she already knew, she whispered back to me, "I know... ya está descansando."

"He's resting now."

The screams that poured out of me didn't even feel like they came from me. They ripped through my body as if I were dying too.

"I knew this could happen. I knew life would change. I knew it would hurt. But what I never knew was how much this painful experience would change me. I didn't know how hard it would be to be a widow with three young kids. And I didn't realize just how much I'd have to change to survive."

The next two weeks were a blur. There was so much family and so many friends in town that I was never truly alone. Christmas Eve and Christmas Day were spent at my house, and honestly, it was nice having so many people there, just the way Douglas always liked it. His funeral was the day before New Year's Eve, and I still remember looking out at all the people in the church before giving my eulogy, blurting out, "Wow, there are a lot of people here." We celebrated New

Year's, and the kids and I even took a short trip to St. Augustine with our best friends before Christmas break ended, and they had to go back to school. That's when reality started to set in, I was now a young widow and a single mom.

My family, friends, and school community were truly amazing. For months, a meal train was organized for us, a shared calendar was set up so I wouldn't be alone at night, groceries were delivered to our door, the kids were taken to their activities, and somehow, our Christmas decorations were even packed away. For weeks, there were plans for us, constant check-ins, and people coming over. They had spent the last sixteen months holding us up so I could focus on my husband. I felt strong. I wasn't crying much or feeling too deeply hurt at that time, but I do remember starting to feel suffocated. Eventually, I told my family and friends they could stop staying overnight. I wanted space.

What I really wanted was for life to go back to how it used to be—before the weekly doctor visits, the research, the dreaded MRI results, the treatments, and before I became a full-time caretaker. I wanted my beautiful life back: being a wife, a mom, a stepmom; having a fulfilling full-time job; spending weekends on the boat; enjoying dinners with friends; having a glass of wine on Friday nights; and spending time with my parents. I convinced myself that if I tried hard enough, I could have that life again, even with one of the most important people missing. I believed I could do it on my own. I felt like I had to prove to everyone that I was fine, that I was strong, that I was doing great.

So, I pushed myself. I quit my job. I booked trips with my kids. I put on a new roof. I organized the house over and over again. I handled the finances, closed out my husband's belongings, kept up with birthdays and family gatherings, and even tried to continue our Thursday dinners with friends, just like we always had. My children were in sports, and I was there in the stands, cheering them on.

On the outside, it looked like I was functioning—smiling, laughing, keeping it all together. But inside, I felt nothing but dread and emptiness, constantly craving life to feel normal again. I thought I looked strong and capable, but the truth was, something kept eating me up. I was dying inside. I hated every second of life. I was in shock. I had no feelings, no dreams. I felt numb. I felt broken.

It started small, but after a few months, things began to slow down. The daily check-in calls, the offers to take my children for a few hours, the help with repairs around the house, the breakfasts, lunches, and dinners, they all began to fade away. Days, sometimes weeks, would pass without anyone coming by. The meals stopped, and everyone returned to their lives. I understood it on some level; despite how much it bothered me.

Then came the hardest blow of all: the relationship with my stepdaughter, my kids' sister, the child I had raised alongside my husband for 11 years, was taken from us. We weren't just grieving my husband and their father; we were grieving her, too. Losing her broke my heart in a way I can't even put into words.

Widowed but not Broken: A Mother's Journey to Community, Strength, and a New Calling.

I didn't have the willpower or strength to move forward. I realized just how bad it was while on a cruise in Europe with my best friends and kids. Surrounded by family and friends, I should've felt grateful. But instead, I hated my life. I was miserable. Every moment reminded me of everything I had lost, including my stepdaughter. I couldn't enjoy anything, not even time with my children.

I was angry and jealous that others could return to their normal lives, laugh without that pit of pain in their stomachs, and keep moving on as if nothing had happened. When they told me they understood, I resented it. How could they? They hadn't lost their person, their hopes, their dreams.

The anger and guilt only grew. I began pushing people away. If I dared to enjoy myself, I feared people would judge me for moving on too quickly. But if I spoke about him too much or cried too openly, I worried I was being a burden.

Anxiety and depression consumed me. I felt alone and insecure. I missed my husband, my best friend, my partner, the father of my kids, the only person who had never made me feel judged. I didn't know how to control the grief. I didn't trust my decisions. And the guilt started eating me up, piece by piece.

Even the people who loved me the most, the ones who had once felt like home, became painful reminders of all I had lost. Deep down, I knew it wasn't their fault. They wanted to help; they wanted the old me back. But she was gone. At the time, I needed someone to be angry at. My anger was all-encompassing. It included Douglas for leaving me too soon, God for taking my husband, and my family and friends for constantly reminding me of my loss at every turn.

When I returned from that cruise, I knew the truth: my old life was gone. I couldn't keep pretending that I could hold on to it. If I didn't make some changes, I was going to lose everything, including my children.

I didn't have a plan, and I wasn't sure where to begin. But looking back now, the choices I made at that time, whether distractions or not the wisest decisions, still helped me survive and slowly find myself again.

Still, three things stand out as the real turning points, the moments that pushed me from simply surviving to actually thriving.

August 20, 2023

The first was joining a gym.

I had always loved working out. My husband and I had a small, personal gym in our garage where we'd work out together. But after he passed, I couldn't bring myself to use it alone. It only reminded me of his absence, of how alone I was. It felt strange because, in the rest of our home, I still felt safe. So instead, I joined a new gym. I didn't know anyone there, but just walking into that place got me out of the house. It gave me a chance to interact with people who knew nothing about me, nothing about my loss or my grieving. There, I could smile, laugh, and simply be, without feeling judged.

I rarely missed a day. Some mornings, I walked in with barely any sleep, sometimes still in tears, but I always showed up. And for that one hour, my anxiety felt lighter, my sadness loosened its grip, and my anger had somewhere to go. It was like a huge burden lifted off my shoulders, and cold water poured into my soul. Slowly, my confidence began to rebuild.

It wasn't about looking good, and it didn't erase my problems, but it changed me, giving me the strength to face them. I became obsessed with going to the gym; I needed that workout to survive most days. Over time, it grew into more than just a release, it became a passion. I started reading constantly about training, the right workouts, and proper nutrition. It gave me something to focus on when my mind wanted to spiral, a sense of control when everything else felt out of control.

I began to open up to the other people at the gym about my life. What started as casual small talk during workouts eventually blossomed into genuine conversations and friendships that grew into lunches, boat rides, group chats, and a support system I never knew I needed.

These women will never fully know how much they've helped me, or how much they continue to help me through what has been the loneliest time of my life.

While Douglas was sick, we were invited by the parents of one of our daughter's friends to attend a prayer group. We went several times as a family, and after Douglas passed, some of the people we had connected with there continued to reach out to me. Little did I know then that those people would become some of my closest friends today.

One of them was Luly B. She invited me to SPARK, an event I had actually gone to a year earlier, just one month before my husband passed. I remembered enjoying it, but at the time I didn't see how it could help me. So, when she suggested I go again, I thought she was crazy. To me, SPARK was for women who wanted to be "boss babes," and that was not me. It had only been eleven months since Douglas's passing, and I had no interest in going back to work or starting a new career. I especially didn't feel comfortable being around accomplished women who seemed to have it all together.

But Luly didn't give up on me. I ended up going to the event again, still not convinced it was for me and with no plans of joining her community afterward. A few weeks later, while we were catching up, I opened up to her about how lost and angry I felt, how I had no direction for what to do next. That's when she asked if I was joining BOOST. I told her no, that I wasn't an entrepreneur and had no plans to become one. She asked me to trust her, saying she felt this could be something good for me. She didn't try to sell me on it. It was her warmth, her honesty, and the way she came across as so genuine that made me say yes. After all, what else did I have to lose?

Widowed but not Broken: A Mother's Journey to Community, Strength, and a New Calling.

At that time, I felt like I was barely surviving. As a single mom, I was overwhelmed, and the only joy I found was during my workouts. Joining the BOOST community pushed me out of my comfort zone. It even got me to dress in something other than gym clothes. It forced me to meet new people who knew nothing about me again. At first, I stayed reserved, but these women didn't let me hide my pain for long. Eventually, I opened up about what brought me there, what my intentions were, and what I hoped to achieve. The truth was, I had one goal: to survive long enough to give my kids a good life while trying not to hate my own.

I believed the life I had planned for my kids would be enough for them.

That was enough for these women to start pushing me. These BOOSTIES started helping me dig deeper into what I truly wanted for myself in the next chapter of my life. I was stepping into a chapter I had never imagined.

I began to look forward to the meetings, even though I wasn't giving my all. I avoided joining a pod because I didn't want to commit and risk letting people down. What I didn't know was that there were other rebels in the group like me, and together we naturally formed a pod of our own.

Being part of this community and meeting these women was a breath of fresh air, reviving, unexpected, and exactly what I didn't know I needed. They leaned in to hear my story. They saw potential in me that I couldn't yet see in myself. They encouraged me to dig deeper, held me accountable, and kept pushing me forward. To this day, they've never given up on me. For the first time, I felt truly seen, not alone, not broken, but understood.

After ten months as a member of the BOOST community, I finally began to see my life more clearly. My goals, my vision, and what truly brought me joy became fully apparent. These women helped me realize that I could turn my love for working out into a business, one that could support women who feel stuck, sad, lonely, or insecure. Just as I was.

It took time to recognize it, but in November 2024, at the BOOST table, they helped me choose a name, guided me through incorporating the company, setting up an Instagram page, and brainstorming logo ideas. With their support, what once felt like only a dream began to take shape. For the first time, I started to truly believe in the life I was creating for myself, for the women I wanted to serve, and for my children.

What amazes me most is that many of these women have become close friends. Some are now my clients. Many have referred me to others. I've also leaned on a few of them for their business expertise. Through this community, I met my therapist, Gilza, who is also part of this book. She has been a steady source of support as I continue finding my way back to myself.

What began as pain is now becoming purpose.

Looking back now, I can honestly say that joining this community was one of the best decisions I could have made, especially during a time when my heart was heavy with grief, and I didn't trust myself to make the right choices.

Over those 10 months, to support my healing journey, I also hired a grief coach and became part of her Brave Widow community. She quickly connected me with another widow in Miami, who has since joined BOOST, now a client of mine, and a dear friend.

My grief coach showed me something I so desperately needed to believe, that it's possible to heal and hurt, or to be hurt and heal, at the same time. She taught me that it's okay to close one chapter of my life while opening another, carrying the blessings of the past with me into the present. And, perhaps most importantly, she taught me how to realize that I could create, on my own, the life I wanted and dreamed of.

The one thing I never truly lost through all of this was my blind faith. I'm not the type of person who reads the Bible or quotes verses, but my prayers were always simple: "God, help me," or "Jesus, I trust in You." Growing up in the Catholic Church, prayer and Mass were regular parts of my life, instilled in me by my parents. Today, I'm so grateful for that foundation. Even though there's still so much I don't understand, this blind faith and hope were the strength that carried me through the painful 16 months my husband was sick.

Douglas and I prayed with the kids often. We took them to church, prayed the rosary together, attended healing Masses, and joined the prayer group. Before his MRIs, I would give him holy water to drink, asking God for a miracle. We didn't receive the miracle we hoped for, but in a way, it's a miracle that I've made it this far.

After Douglas passed, though, I found it difficult to go to church or even pray the rosary. But I never stopped praying. In the darkest moments, when anxiety took over or sleep wouldn't come, I would whisper prayers from my heart. The Hail Mary became my comfort, and I would recite it over and over again. Slowly, a sense of calm would begin to settle over me, accompanied by a fragile but growing hope that somehow, someway, I was going to make it through this and be okay again. I didn't know how or when, but I trusted in that hope.

Through the prayer group and my kids' community, we became close friends with Betsy and her family. Betsy is also part of this book and the BOOST community and has been a wonderful friend and connection.

She and her family had experienced a heartbreaking loss, yet she never gave up hope. I remember thinking, if this woman can hold on to joy after everything she's been through, why can't I? My heart longed to feel sincere joy again. I wanted to be the kind of mom who was present, who cherished the small moments. I wanted to laugh with my family and friends without the heaviness of grief weighing on my heart.

Widowed but not Broken: A Mother's Journey to Community, Strength, and a New Calling.

Betsy, who had introduced me to my grief coach, also helped me discover the wonders of the Blessed Sacrament, a place I now visit regularly. I take time to journal there, praying for peace and guidance. During countless moments of anxiety, or whenever I needed to process my thoughts, I would call her. She always reminded me to lean into my faith and to ask the Holy Spirit for peace. She'd say, "If it doesn't bring you peace, then it's not meant for you." So, I prayed often—and still do.

I had already gained strength and resilience through working out. I had regained confidence and trust in myself by joining the BOOST community and rediscovering who I truly was. But now, more than ever, I knew I had to rely on my faith to carry me through the hardest days ahead: to push me forward when I felt like giving up, to help my children heal, and to remind me to appreciate my blessings while finding peace and joy again.

This journey led me to SoulCore, a movement that blends prayer with core strengthening and functional movement, nourishing both body and soul. My sister first introduced me to it, and later Betsy, who became certified, shared it with me more deeply. Recently, I joined and became a certified SoulCore instructor myself. It's now part of my business, a way to share my passion for faith and fitness while helping other women find strength, peace, and healing.

Through this journey, I've learned that no matter how deep the pain runs, healing and rebuilding are possible. I went from feeling broken and numb, just trying to survive, to slowly rediscovering confidence in the gym, hope in my faith, and purpose in the communities around me. I've learned that joy in motherhood can return, even after unimaginable loss. And I've learned that healing isn't about returning to the life I once had, it's about stepping into the new life I was meant to live, one built on strength, faith, and the courage to keep moving forward.

I'm still healing, but I can now enjoy my children in ways I never imagined when I first began this journey. I am deeply grateful for my family and friends who stood by me with unwavering patience as I navigated through this process. I'm also thankful for the new women who have entered my life, becoming an essential part of my healing. Above all, I'm incredibly thankful for my children; my why, my anchor. They have walked beside me with love and patience as I've healed, and their strength has been the greatest gift of all.

I've faced many setbacks, and there were moments when I stumbled. But each challenge taught me invaluable lessons. I've learned how to confront difficulties, keep moving forward, and trust myself once again. I am no longer just surviving, I am becoming.

Today, I walk alongside women who feel stuck, lonely, or unsure of where to begin, helping them reconnect with their strength through movement, community, and faith-based practices. If you're ready to take even the smallest step toward rediscovering who you are, I would be honored to walk with you.

About the Author

Hi, I'm Luly Cordoba—a mom, widow, and personal trainer who turned my deepest heartbreak into a journey of strength, healing, and purpose.

Formerly a professional in the corporate world, my life shifted when I lost my husband to cancer and, with his loss, contact with my stepdaughter. Choosing to find joy again, I took a leap of faith and started my own business, channeling my passion into BeLulyFIT—a space where women find strength, healing, and community.

In this chapter, you'll get a glimpse of how I found community, how connecting with other women helped me feel seen and understood, and how putting myself first through fitness and faith gave me the strength to move forward and feel joy again for myself and my children. My journey is one of deep loss, but also of hope—showing that you are not alone, that healing is possible, and that you can step into a life of confidence, purpose, and strength.

When I'm not coaching, you'll find me boating with my children or enjoying a sporting event.

Follow my journey: **@mrslulyfcordoba**

Chapter 6

FINDING HER LIGHT AGAIN AND SHINING BRIGHTER THAN EVER

BY BARBIE GARCIA

"How did I even get here?" That was the question that I kept asking myself. Everything was a whirlwind and by the time I realized it, I was already lost in every way a person can be.

I had fallen into the darkest place of my life. It felt like a tunnel with no end, no way forward, no way back. The air was heavy, pressing against me, making it hard to breathe. Every step I tried to take only echoed back emptier than the last. The walls pressed in, swallowing every ounce of hope I once carried.

There was no flicker, no glow, no hint of the so-called light at the end. Only blackness.

It was disorienting. Paralyzing. Like being trapped inside my own body, buried alive while still standing. That was my tunnel. And for a long time, I truly believed I would never find a way out. I was crushed all the way to my core; to the depths of my soul. The pain I was feeling blinded me physically, emotionally, mentally and spiritually. I didn't know who I was anymore. I couldn't move. I couldn't think. I had lost everything: my faith, my hope, my LIGHT… and eventually, I lost ME.

It started with heartbreak—the kind that knocks the wind out of you and makes the world feel unfamiliar overnight. The kind that comes with betrayal—the discovery that the person you trusted most is not who you thought they were. One moment, I thought I had love, stability, and a future to build on and the next, it was gone. The silence after the goodbye echoed louder than the words that ended us. At first, it was just the pain of losing someone I loved, but then it spread into everything else. It turned into the loss of everything I dreamed of, worked so hard for, wanted and believed I deserved. I felt like a soldier trained for war, only to be told to surrender before I even had a chance to fight. I hated that feeling. It wasn't in me to simply give up.

This wasn't just about losing love. It was about losing myself. Heartbreak was the ignition, but the breakdown was the wildfire that followed, burning through parts of me I thought were untouchable. Suddenly, getting out of bed felt heavy. The things that once made me smile didn't even register. I went through the motions of life, but inside I was fading. My mind never stopped racing. My body was exhausted.

And no matter how many times I told myself to "snap out of it," I couldn't.

Each day blurred into the next, heavy and hollow. It wasn't just sadness—it felt as if the ground had opened beneath me, and every part of who I was collapsed into the void. It was like watching the demolition of a building—loud, violent, and unstoppable. One moment I was standing, holding myself together with fragile walls and shaky foundations, and the next, everything came crashing down. The parts of me I thought were solid—my confidence, my sense of direction, my hope—crumbled into dust. There was nothing quiet or graceful about it. It was messy, chaotic, and it left me buried in the wreckage, staring at pieces I didn't know how to put back together. And just like a demolition, the real ache wasn't only in what was destroyed. It was about facing the empty space left behind and wondering if I'd ever find the strength to rebuild.

I felt completely alone. No one could possibly understand what I was going through. It felt wrong and unfair. I was angry, bitter and yet I kept showing up for everyone else, even though I couldn't show up for myself. I still don't know how I managed that. Somehow, I was holding up the light for others while I couldn't find my own. At least, that's how it felt then; like my flame had gone. It was as if my very soul was shutting down. I was drowning in emotions I didn't even recognize. They consumed me. I was living in a reality that didn't feel like mine, a life that no longer fit who I was, and I was desperate to escape it.

Asking for help was not an option. Vulnerability felt like weakness, and weakness was unacceptable. I had always been strong, courageous, the one who figured things out, who carried the weight without asking anyone to share it. For the first time, I believed I had lost my resilience. I was numb, lost, and captured by my own circumstances. I was ashamed that I had allowed myself to fall this far. Deep down, I knew this couldn't be what the rest of my life was meant to look like. But the truth was, I had no idea how to move forward.

Even in the ruins, though, something stirred. In all that emptiness, I found the faintest spark, the part of me that refused to stay buried. Rising again was not graceful, and it was anything but quick. The process was slow, messy, and painful. I had to learn how to stand all over again, shaky and unsure. Each small step forward was a quiet rebellion against the darkness; proof that even after everything had crumbled, I could rebuild. The crushing I thought was the end began to reveal itself as a beginning. It was the painful clearing of everything false, making room for a stronger foundation; one built on truth, resilience, and a light I thought I had lost, but had only been waiting to be reignited.

At the time, I couldn't understand that the process I was going through was part of the journey to my destination. I resented every second of it. The wait was unbearable. I kept asking God why this was happening and how long it would last. It's almost ironic that my favorite Bible verse has always been Psalm 46:10, which reads "Be still and know that I am God." Back then, I couldn't be still. I couldn't know. I couldn't see God or feel Him anymore. I felt abandoned, even betrayed. Yet in that silence, His message became clearer: You are exactly where you need to be. In the stillness, I began to learn the value of surrender. Surrender wasn't defeat; it was release. It was letting go of what I thought my life should look like, and opening my heart to what could be.

I realized I couldn't just wait for life to change on its own; I had to take part in my own healing. I had to choose to show up for myself, even when it felt impossible. I had to start shaping the life I wanted, the life I was created and destined for. That meant being intentional, staying committed, and being loyal to the vision of my future. It meant taking small, aligned steps, one after another, until I could feel myself rising again. I had to reclaim my life. I had to be the one to light the way back to ME.

My transformation from breakdown to breakthrough began with Dr. Betsy Guerra. I had been following Betsy for some time and had wanted to work with her for a while, but felt I wasn't ready. Truth is, we're rarely "ready" for the things that end up changing us the most. When she announced the launch of her Faith-Based Coaching Academy, I felt a pull that I could not ignore. Despite my doubts, and my unraveling faith, I knew this was my calling. Coaching wasn't just something I wanted to do, it was what I was born to do. I decided: I'm going to do this. I will make this happen!

I still remember the first day of class. One by one, people introduced themselves, sharing who they were and why they had joined the cohort. When it came to me, the words wouldn't come. Instead, the tears did. Through those tears, I asked, "How can I help others when my life is in shambles?" Betsy looked at me with such kindness and said words that I will never forget: "That is the perfect moment to help people." Her words sank deep. My brokenness wasn't a barrier; it was a bridge. It was the very thing that would connect me to others.

I poured myself into the program, even though I was still walking through one of the darkest seasons of my life. Fast forward, I pushed through and graduated with flying colors! I wasn't just a Master's-level social worker anymore. I was now a Certified Life Coach. But even more than that, I was a woman who had survived "the tunnel" and discovered that the light inside me had never truly gone out. It had only been waiting for me to turn back toward it.

Along the way, community found me. Through Betsy, I met inspiring women like Caroline de Posada, Luly B, and so many others who radiate wisdom, passion, and purpose. Each connection opened new doors, new perspectives, and new possibilities. My relationship with Betsy wasn't just another connection—it was a catalyst that shifted the trajectory of my journey and expanded my world in ways I could have never imagined.

A few months after graduating from the Faith-Based Coaching Academy, I heard about Luly B's event, SPARK. I thought it was a great invitation to a powerful experience and I decided to register. However, I paid my ticket… and then never showed up. A whole year passed, and the event came back up on my radar. I decided to grab a seat at Betsy's table and made myself a promise: no excuses, no backing out, I would show up, rain or shine.

That day was transformational. It wasn't just an event; it was a turning point. The theme was "Go For It," and I couldn't been more fitting for me. I knew I had to stop shrinking, second-guessing, and waiting for the "right" moment. It was time to step fully into the opportunities God had already placed in front of me. The message lit a fire inside me. My dreams weren't out of reach; they were waiting for me on the other side of courage. That day, I chose to go for it. And from that moment on, everything began to shift.

When Luly introduced her BOOST community, I felt that this was supposed to be my next step. It was as if my soul remembered what it was always meant to do: spread its wings, embrace the light, and soar toward the life that had been waiting for me all along. It reminded me of the power of showing up for myself and choosing to step into the spaces where my light could grow brighter. My heart whispered, "It's time." Without hesitation, I joined BOOST. I didn't think I was ready. I wasn't sure it was for me. But it turned out to be one of the best decisions of my life.

Community has presented me with opportunities I never could have created on my own. It opened doors I didn't even know existed—opportunities for growth, healing, connection, and for becoming more of who I was meant to be. When I couldn't lift myself, community lifted me. In moments when I felt broken and unseen, they reflected back the strength I couldn't recognize in myself. They showed me that the light we carry grows brighter when we share it, and that courage is often borrowed until we can stand on our own again. I discovered that every conversation can plant a seed, every connection can spark a possibility, and every act of support can shift the course of a life.

From the ashes of heartbreak and breakdown, I discovered the truth that even in my darkest moments, there was still a light inside of me waiting to be reignited. Piece by piece, I rebuilt not into who I was before, but into someone stronger, clearer, and more alive. The ashes became soil for new growth, and the ruins became the foundation for a life lit with purpose. What once felt like destruction revealed itself as transformation, a reminder that no matter how deeply we fall apart, we always hold the power to rise again. That realization changed everything. I understood that even in the darkest seasons, the light inside us never truly disappears - it simply waits for us to choose it, nurture it, and let it shine once again.

Looking back, I can honestly say I am thankful for the trials that once felt like the end of me. In truth, they were the beginning. What I once resented was the very thing that prepared me. My pain became purpose. My breakdown became breakthrough. Because of it, I don't just understand pain; I also understand transformation. And now, I have the honor of walking beside others, guiding them as they navigate their own tunnels, reminding them that their light, too, has never left – it is only waiting to be reignited.

If you are in a dark place right now, hear me when I say this: you are not forgotten. Let my story remind you that there is always hope. You were not born to live in darkness, and neither was I. I know what it feels like to wonder if you'll ever make it through. But here's the truth: you will. Pain does not come to destroy you. It comes to shape you. It teaches, it refines, and when you are ready to release it, it leaves. Healing hurts, but healing also builds.

You are stronger than you realize. Even in the silence of your struggle, the light inside you is waiting to return. Hold on, breathe, and trust that one day you'll look back and see that this darkness was not your undoing—it was your becoming.

It is time to write a new story. Not tomorrow. Not when everything feels perfect. Today. Take that first step forward into possibility. Seek out community. Healing doesn't happen in isolation—it happens when we allow ourselves to be seen, supported, and loved. Community reminds us of our light when we've forgotten it. It holds us up when standing feels impossible, and where encouragement flows in when our hope runs low.

You don't need another plan, another checklist, or another reason to wait. What you need is permission to rise. You were created to feel alive, lit from the inside out, and connected to the truth of who you are. You don't have to settle for heaviness or numbness. You were made for more. Sometimes, all it takes is one spark, one shift, one brave decision to reignite the fire within you.

You can choose joy.

You can choose light.

You can choose you.

Reignite your light!

Reclaim your life!

This is the BOOST your soul has been waiting for!

About the Author

Hi! I'm Barbie Garcia, a Certified Life Coach with a heart for helping others reignite the light within themselves. My mission is to guide people through the dark tunnels of doubt, heartbreak, and fear—and lead them into a life filled with clarity, joy, and renewed purpose.

My journey to coaching was born out of my own transformation. After walking through a season of breakdown and feeling completely lost, I reached a pivotal moment where I chose not to stay in the darkness any longer. That decision became the spark that reignited my light. Today, I share my story openly to remind you that no matter how dim life may feel, the light is never gone—it can always be reclaimed.

Drawing from both my personal journey and my professional training, I bring a blend of empathy, insight, and practical tools to every session. Through one-on-one coaching, I empower others to shift their mindset, embrace healing, and step fully into the life they were created to live.

When I'm not coaching, you'll find me singing, dancing, spending time with my loved ones, reading books that inspire me, or simply enjoying life's little joys.

I hope my story encourages you to believe in your own light and inspires you to take that next brave step toward the life you truly deserve. My message is simple yet powerful: *Reignite your light. Reclaim your life.*

Let's walk together as you step into your light! You can find me on Instagram **[@YourInfiniteLight]**. Your breakthrough begins today!

Chapter 7

FROM TRAUMA TO TRIUMPH: THE POWER OF AWARENESS AND HEALING IN COMMUNITY

BY DANIELA MOUNTS

At the end of 2018, I launched a nonprofit for young Latino entrepreneurs. At the same time, I was juggling a demanding job and struggling to piece myself back together after yet another rock bottom in my marriage.

Then the phone rang. A woman's sweet voice greeted me on the other end, telling me I'd received the President's Volunteer Gold Award from the White House. A call like that should've lifted me to the sky or make me feel on top of the world.

After all, doing good work is never about recognition, but when you pour your heart into something, being seen, being acknowledged, it's like a quiet confirmation that what you're doing matters. But, oddly enough, all I felt was numb.

Just eight years earlier, at Christmas 2010, I had moved to the United States with my husband and daughter. I remember sitting at the airport, overwhelmed by the vastness of it all, like something straight out of the movies. It was big, colorful, full of promise and possibility. And yet, when I glanced down at my wallet, I realized I barely had a few hundred dollars to my name, half of which was already earmarked for my husband's family Christmas gifts.

Soon after the holiday season faded, reality settled in. We lived in a tiny apartment, scraping by on a $25,000 household income, weighed down by unresolved wounds, infidelity, and my drinking.

A year later, I received my paperwork and joined a tech company. For the next decade, I threw myself into work. I was determined to succeed, and despite the odds, I finished school, built a career, and climbed a trajectory that surprised everyone, including me.

I was so grateful for the opportunities, but gratitude alone couldn't fill the emptiness in my soul.

"SOY EMPRENDEDOR"

The night I thought of the name for my non-profit, *"Soy Emprendedor"* (I am an entrepreneur), I couldn't sleep. I was so excited, I could hardly keep still. The next morning, everything just clicked. I jumped into creating the marketing materials, building the website; it all came together so naturally. It felt like everything I'd ever wanted to do was right in front of me, waiting for me to grab it.

In just a week, I was ready to share my idea with the world. My heart raced with excitement, my skin tingling with goosebumps. For the first time, I thought, *this is it. I've found my purpose.* Or at least, that's what I believed.

> "Only those with a growth mindset truly pay attention to information that can stretch their understanding."
> "People with a growth mindset don't just look for challenges, they thrive in them."
>
> — Carol Dweck

Running your own organization, no matter how big or small, requires the same amount of time, energy, and heart. I'll never forget the words of my boss during my tech days: *"A show for one person, ten, or ten thousand takes the same dedication to make it successful."* Those words stayed with me, especially when it came to building something meaningful. They hold just as true for growing ideas as they did for any project I worked on. I'm forever grateful for her mentorship.

Soy Emprendedor became more than just a program to me; it became a sanctuary where we could teach entrepreneurship, the growth mindset, grit, and resilience. The foundation of the program was inspired by a book I had read long before the term *"mindset"* was tossed around on social media: Mindset by Carol Dweck. Over time, more than forty incredible students walked through those doors, all supported by countless volunteers and mentors who gave their time and shared their wisdom. I wasn't just proud of the program itself; I was in awe of the students' courage, their willingness to show up, to learn, to fail, and to try again. I was equally moved by the community that blossomed around them.

But what meant the most to me, what I will always treasure, is the role I played as their coach. To be entrusted with their growth, to be a part of their journey, was a gift I will carry with me forever.

Up until that moment, I had lived much of my life behind the scenes. Whether in my personal or professional life, I found ways to stay hidden. I worked hard behind a computer, or stood quietly behind my husband's achievements, sometimes because it felt safer, and other times, because I chose it. Playing small became my comfort zone.

But running a nonprofit was different. It demanded something more; prayer, trust, and an endless stream of asking. Asking students to believe in the program, praying parents would remember to bring their kids, requesting for grants, and reaching out for volunteers and resources.

A mission like that strips you down to your core. There's no hiding behind titles or other people's success. It's just you, standing there, fully exposed. No screens, no distractions, only the raw truth of what you are doing. And that truth, in all its vulnerability, was both terrifying and freeing. For the first time, I couldn't shrink away or hide behind anyone else's success. I had to stand tall and claim my own.

> *"You will continue to attract the same patterns, people, and situations until you learn the lesson your soul came here to learn."*
>
> **- Gary Zukav**

The night before receiving the award, I shot upright in bed at 2 a.m., gasping for air. I screamed, pleading for someone to take me to the hospital. My husband quickly shoved me into the shower, trying to ground me. It was in that moment, drenched in fear, that I realized I had never known life without this constant undercurrent of panic. This wasn't the first time anxiety had seized my body, and I knew it wouldn't be the last.

Even though I felt like I was achieving so much at the time but that didn't stop my panic attacks. There were moments when I couldn't move, I felt paralyzed, and couldn't speak. Despite creating a playground, a platform where I could bring my whole self to others, all my hidden fears and triggers seemed to surface. The more I tried to change my thoughts, the stronger the anxiety gripped me. I questioned whether I deserved the recognition, wondered if I was truly making a difference. I felt like an imposter, like I was failing at the very heart of the work I had built.

And then, the world stopped. Really stopped.

COVID

When I got COVID, there were days I truly thought I was dying. I couldn't even put together an email. For the first time, I just stopped caring about everything; what my family would think, my projects, my goals. And even if I tried to care, I couldn't. I was forced to sit with my thoughts, to confront the things I'd been avoiding. And, as it often happens, the uninvited thoughts showed up at my door, unannounced.

I spent months in bed, the world outside feeling distant. I cried for things I hadn't let myself cry for in years. I cried because I couldn't breathe, which only made my anxiety spiral. But strangely, I also cried because it felt good; too good, like a release I didn't know I needed. I cried for my sister, for the grief I'd buried deep when she passed. I cried for the secret wounds I'd kept hidden for so long, the ones from my childhood that no one ever saw. I cried for the small loss; half of my front tooth, gone from one careless moment while drinking (and now, I can laugh about it). I cried for the pain that seeped through the years of my marriage. And, above all, I cried for the beautiful parts of me that seemed to disappear somewhere along the way.

> *"Your trauma is not your identity. It's the soil from which your strength, wisdom, and compassion can grow."*
>
> — **Unknown**

From Trauma to Triumph:
The Power of Awareness and Healing in Community

INHALE, EXHALE...

One year of being so sick changed the course of my life in ways I never saw coming. I found myself walking into a yoga studio, initially out of curiosity. What started as a simple interest quickly spiraled into what I jokingly called "certificatitis", signing up for every training, every workshop, reading every book I could get my hands on. Yoga, but more importantly, ancient wisdom and faith, became something far beyond study. It became a reflection of who I was.

Suddenly, every mentor, every experience, both the good and the bad, began to fit together like pieces of a puzzle I hadn't even realized I'd been working on for years. That's when I truly understood: numbness and healing are not the same thing.

It wasn't that I hadn't tried before to "become better." But this time, something was different. I allowed myself to get uncomfortable, to stop avoiding the pain. I looked inward, with a new perspective, facing my experiences, my shadows, my traumas, and my blessings, all at once. Especially the painful ones. They stopped being scars I was ashamed of and became teachers. Each one showed me something about myself I had been unwilling to see.

With awareness, time, and practice, I learned to manage my panic attacks using breathing and meditation. Through that, I began to reframe my story. Instead of asking "Why did this happen to me?" I started asking, "What am I meant to learn from this?" That simple shift was powerful. It felt like stepping into my own power, taking ownership, and no longer giving it away to people, places, or circumstances.

Uplifting others has always been a part of me. From a young age, I longed for connection, and I always found myself part of some community. As a teenager, it was through my Catholic church, and I even ran my first summer camp for neighborhood kids. When I helped others feel happy, supported them, and made sure they were achieving their goals, I felt whole.

Putting others first sounds like a noble idea, even a moment that feels very "Jesus-like." It's the kind of thing that can make you feel good for a while, but I ended up putting my own needs last. I didn't have healthy boundaries, and I hid behind accomplishments, thinking they would somehow make up for it. But in doing so, I lost all joy. For those of us who've experienced trauma, avoidance becomes our go-to survival tool. But avoidance is just a sensory memory, it doesn't go away. The distractions; work, alcohol (I've been sober for 12 years now), became my defense mechanisms, much like the way people multitask to escape what's truly there. But eventually, something big happens, and that loop you're stuck in won't stop. The grief, delayed and buried, comes to the surface once the distractions lose their power.

Looking back, I can see the small moments where I held myself back, hesitating to ask for a promotion, feeling upset by a friend's outgoing personality. I realize now that I was holding all the answers inside me, but I couldn't see them at the time. My inadequacies and painful experiences, they didn't just hold me back; they also shone a light on who I truly was, and illuminating my core essence.

Paradoxically, trauma became one of my greatest teachers. When I wasn't in survival mode, when I kept quiet, I learned to observe. The doubts, the thoughts that something was wrong with me, sparked a curiosity. It led me to understand others better, to feel their energy, and to ask questions instead of jumping to conclusions.

That curiosity gave birth to my creativity. It guided me into building my work, step by step. I didn't continue with my nonprofit, but that was a blueprint I created, a way to face my own weaknesses, a challenge I had no choice but to meet. Walking away from it all finally revealed something I'd been avoiding for years: the wounds I carried with me, even into the things I cared about the most.

But in that moment, when I allowed myself to see me with compassion, it clicked. I finally realized that, deep down, it wasn't just about helping others. *I wanted to save myself. I wanted to be loved. I wanted to be seen.*

> *"The mind is everything. What you think you become."*
>
> **– Buddha**

Today, as a business owner and Life Coach, looking back on the many drafts of my mission, I can tell you from the bottom of my heart that healing and finding clarity is deeply personal. It's not an easy road, but I can also tell you, with all certainty, that the answers are already within you.

Yes, trauma and bad experiences are painful; and sometimes, unbearable. But as you work through them, as you decode and peel back those layers, it's important to take your time. You need to find spaces and people who can help your soul speak, people who will hold space for you. It's okay to ask for help and guidance.

Building your intuition and nurturing your faith is the most vital skill you'll ever cultivate. It's a lifelong journey, a constant practice of learning to love and accept yourself. When life feels out of control, that's when your inner strength becomes your anchor, allowing you to continue embracing both your strengths and your flaws. Over time, you'll find balance and grow into the fullest version of yourself.

With love and intention, I want to share the foundational steps I used to heal and grow:

Awareness was my first step. I had to learn to see my most painful experiences as sources of wisdom and strength. I started recognizing the patterns that had kept me small, saying yes when I really wanted to say no, holding back my voice in rooms where I should have spoken up.

Faith came next. I had to learn to create space for the unseen. No matter what you believe in, it's those small, daily practices that make all the difference. For me, my Bible was the only thing that kept me afloat during my darkest days. When it feels like you're inadequate, remember this scripture of the Bible that says,

From Trauma to Triumph:
The Power of Awareness and Healing in Community

Be strong and courageous. Do not be afraid; do not be discouraged, for the Lord your God will be with you wherever you go."

– Joshua 1:9

It's a journey, not a race. Healing didn't happen in one big moment, it unfolded in dozens of small, awkward, and imperfect steps.

Gratitude didn't erase the pain, but it kept the pain from being the only thing I heard. I'm deeply thankful for my family, my parents, my mentors, my friends, and for my boss who saw me when I couldn't see myself.

Giving is just as important as receiving. It's essential to fill your own cup first. That's the heart of community. I saw it in the nonprofit I built, in the retreats I attended, and in every circle of healing I joined. This is what balance looks like.

CELEBRATE YOUR PROGRESS.

Every stumble taught me something valuable. Every tiny victory mattered. When I look back, those small steps became the solid foundation for everything I stand on today.

FINDING YOUR TRIBE

Finding your tribe is one of the most important things you can do for yourself. But finding the right community is just as crucial, it can lift you up or hold you back. And it's okay to outgrow a community.

As you search, take time to ask yourself: *Is this the right fit for me? What's missing? Am I showing up for myself and others the way I want to?* Do this with kindness, love, and patience.

LULY B'S COMMUNITY

I found the missing piece of the puzzle in Luly B's community. It's the reason I'm able to share even this small part of my story. And here's what I've learned: being saved, loved, and truly seen starts with showing up for yourself. It's about being real with others, even when you're still figuring things out. You don't have to have all the answers. You don't even have to feel like you've got it together. But you do need to let people know who you are, what you're working on, and where you need help, even when it feels like you're Inadequate.

The truth is, if you hide away, stay silent, or try not to make others uncomfortable, they'll never know how to show up for you. The right people, the ones meant to walk with you, will know how to meet you where you are.

Life's challenges will keep coming. Family, friends, coworkers, they all bring their own personalities, agendas, and intentions. And though they can shape your world. However, having the right people by your side is what matters most. Knowing where your strengths lie is important, but understanding where your weaknesses are, that's even more crucial.

About the Author

Daniela Mounts is a Certified Life Coach, business owner, and brand strategist with expertise in storytelling, graphic design, marketing, and communications that drive measurable results and organizational growth. Over the past fifteen years, she has worked across diverse industries, including technology, data analytics, aerospace, and nonprofits.

Recognized for her commitment to entrepreneurship and education, Daniela founded a nonprofit organization for Latino students, earning the President's Volunteer Gold Service Award from The White House and the Governor's Volunteer Award of North Carolina. She also holds multiple wellness and coaching certifications, including one from the Jay Shetty Certification School, and is a co-owner of a sports fashion brand.

Having worked with everyone from C-level executives to operations teams—and even on the yoga mat—Daniela has learned one truth: titles don't define us; our calling does. She integrates spiritual and wellness strategies, proven methodologies, and her professional background to guide leaders, entrepreneurs, and growth-driven individuals. Over the past decade, she has lived and applied the very tools she now shares with her clients—bringing structure, clarity, and sustainable results aligned with both professional success and personal fulfillment.

→ **Ready to bring structure to your vision and grow with intention?**

Book a session here:
https://calendly.com/kdanielamounts/discovery-call

Connect with Daniela:

- Instagram: @danielamounts
- Website: www.danielamounts.com
- Email: contact@danielamounts.com

Chapter 8

STYLED FOR MORE: A WOMAN'S JOURNEY OF SURVIVAL, AWAKENING, AND POWER

BY MEI JORGE

BEFORE THE CLOSET GOT HEAVY

Click. Click. Click. My heels echoed down the hallway of a corporate office in Miami, blazer sharp, confidence high. Back then, I didn't know that the woman I was — the one who matched her earrings to her mood and booked flights on a whim — would one day feel like a stranger to me. Before the diapers, the deadlines, and the endless dishes… there was her. There was me.

If you scrolled far enough back on my camera roll, you'd find her — the woman who traveled the world with her husband, swiped on bold lipstick like armor, and had time to curl her hair just because. She didn't drink her coffee cold unless it was on purpose. She knew where her passport was at all times, and her closet had outfits for every kind of mood.

That woman was me.

I was a graphic designer, a proud holder of a BA from the University of Miami and an MBA from FIU. Yes, I collected degrees and paychecks like frequent flyer miles. For ten years, I was part of the marketing team at a top healthcare system. My work wasn't just "designing" — it was the billboards along I-95, the presentations that landed ideas in boardrooms. My nights? They were filled with dinners out or planning the next trip.

Style was part of it, too. My office wear wasn't just about clothes — it was a daily ritual, a way to express myself, a rhythm that grounded me. Some mornings, it was a polished blouse; other days, a necklace that pulled it all together. Clothes weren't just fabric — they were little reminders that I belonged. The way you show up visually can reflect how you feel inside. And if you're wondering where to start? For me, it was lipstick. For you, it might be your favorite heels, or the song that makes you dance in the kitchen. Whatever it is, do it.

Back then, I had no idea this simple gift would become part of my calling. Just like I pieced together outfits that made me feel unstoppable, one day I would help women pull together wardrobes, spaces, and brand graphics that reminded them they already were.

A few years into my career, I married. My husband and I became wanderlusters with passports full of stamps. We visited each of the

Seven Wonders of the World — and then some. Tokyo's neon hum. The sun rising over the Nile. The ancient temples of Angkor Wat in Cambodia. Bought scarves from markets where no one spoke English. Each trip wasn't just an escape; it was a masterclass that later shaped my closet.

I thought I'd keep climbing the corporate ladder forever, but even then, cracks were forming. When I realized I wouldn't have the opportunity to grow professionally where I was, I accepted my mom's offer to take over the family business — a primary care doctor's office. It wasn't my dream, but the money was tempting. So I stepped in, kept the doors open, and suddenly found myself doing it all — managing staff, running operations, and yes, even making sure the brochures didn't look like they'd been designed in Microsoft Word. But the truth? It never fulfilled me.

Scrubs replaced silk. Sneakers replaced heels. And with each morning in polyester, I felt myself shrinking. Drowning in shapeless uniforms, I longed for color, fabric, style — anything that reminded me I was more than a walking pharmacy poster. So, I carved out a secret rebellion: a style blog I called *Blame it on Mei*. My camera became my mirror, my posts my runway, my outfits my protest.

At first, it was just about sharing my style and tips. But let's be honest — it also fed my need for connection. Those little hearts? They weren't just likes — they were proof that I wasn't invisible.

After three years of running the office, the physician passed away from old age. I took it as the perfect excuse to close the doors and walk away from a business that had never really felt like mine. To be honest, it was terrifying. I had no safety net — just a blog, my voice, and the hope that someone was listening. From that moment on, I dove fully into content creation — not because it was easy, but because for the first time, it felt like me.

What had started as a side project had turned into something real, something alive. It was the spark I didn't know I'd been missing. And to my surprise, brands started noticing *Blame it on Mei*. Big names — Dove, Macy's, Neutrogena, Sephora, and more. Each collaboration wasn't just a paycheck — it was proof that my creativity mattered.

Through content creation, I also found a community of creatives who "got it" — women who were building something online, just like me. I became a leader in that circle, and soon enough, I was the one on stage at local and national conferences.

Standing in front of crowds, sharing the kind of wisdom you don't find in a textbook: late nights YouTubing WordPress' how-tos, becoming besties with Google over SEO headaches, and flipping 'gifted' brand deals into paid ones by pitching like my mortgage depended on it. I felt like I was in my element.I wasn't nervous — I thrived in the spotlight. I loved being the "expert," guiding others with everything I had learned. It was the first time I felt fully seen — not just for what I wore, but for the voice behind it.

Life was big, and I was fully alive in it. Or so I thought.

But here's the truth no one tells you — sometimes what looks like aliveness is just a performance. Sometimes what looks like confidence is really just armor. Maybe your armor wasn't lipstick before a meeting, like mine. Maybe it was dry shampoo on third-day hair, or a smile that didn't reach your heart, but you wore it anyway.

I didn't realize then, how quickly the weight of motherhood would start stripping everything away piece by piece, until the woman I once was, seemed to fade into the background.

Do you remember who you were before life started weighing you down?

THE WEIGHT I WORE

Motherhood didn't come in softly. No — it hit me like a bright fluorescent light flicked on at midnight: blinding, hard to ignore. And just when I thought I could catch my breath, it happened again. Twice. Twice the love, twice the chaos, twice the unraveling of who I thought I was.

Suddenly, the woman who used to plan outfits for vacations was standing in a cluttered kitchen, trying to negotiate with a toddler about which cup would avoid a meltdown. *"Not the blue cup, Mamá. The other blue. No, not that one."* (Yes, apparently, there are a thousand shades of blue.)

The weight on my shoulders wasn't just from carrying babies — two under two, to be exact. It was the never-ending grocery lists. The pediatrician appointments. The mental tabs that were always open: milk, diapers, patience, time. And somewhere in all those tabs, my marriage started to feel like just another task to manage. I became the household COO for everyone.

I was on autopilot. Wake, feed, clean, repeat. I told myself this was just motherhood — everyone else seemed to handle it, so I should too.

My style had become a reflection of everything I was: leggings, simple tops, flats. Getting dressed wasn't about joy anymore — it was about survival. On the rare nights we managed a date, they felt less like romance and more like strategy sessions: who's scheduling the home repairs, what errands still hadn't been done, and who was simply too tired to keep talking.

One afternoon, I locked myself in the bathroom, claiming I needed to "brush my teeth." I sat on the closed toilet lid, letting the fan cover my sobs. There was dried spit-up on my shoulder, cold coffee waiting on the counter, and tiny fists pounding at the door. *"Mamá?"* A small voice called. I stared at my reflection — puffy eyes, unbrushed hair, a face that barely looked like mine anymore. Forget spa facials. My signature look was exhaustion with a side of dry shampoo. And then the thought I was too afraid to admit slipped in: Is this all there is?

But every now and then, I'd rebel. A swipe of bright lipstick, so bold it might've scared the UPS guy. A pair of colorful pants that screamed, *"I'm still here."* And on those days? Things were different. The tantrums didn't disappear, but I felt like I could face them with a little more strength. I felt… closer to the woman I used to be.

I invite you to pick one small act today that reminds you of who you are — wear your favorite color, slip into those favorite heels, or blast a song that stirs something inside you.

Most of the time, I sacrificed my time, my spark, and my sense of self. Little by little, I stopped being the main character in my own life and became nothing more than background noise.

Do you ever look back at old photos of yourself and wonder, where did she go? I wondered the same. I missed her so much, the woman who felt truly alive. But she was buried beneath diapers, dishes, and the mental load no one else could see. The hardest part? I couldn't find a way out, not yet.

Of course, there were moments of beauty, birthdays, first steps, baby giggles that could melt even the deepest exhaustion. But beneath it all, I still felt like a supporting character in my own story.

Through it all, I kept holding on to *Blame it on Mei* — the captions, the camera, the heels waiting in my closet — because it wasn't just a blog. It was my way of holding onto the part of me that was still there.

And here's what I figured out much later — losing touch with your style isn't about fashion. It's about losing touch with yourself. That's why, today, when I style women, it's not about getting more clothes. It's about helping them reconnect with the woman they forgot was still inside.

Do you ever feel like you've disappeared in your own life?

STYLED FOR AWAKENING

Here's the thing about survival mode: it can be tricky. You don't always realize you're in it until something cracks open the door and lets the light in. For me, that light came in flickers.

One of those first flickers? Spark 2023. My therapist, Gilza — fun fact, she's also writing a chapter in this book — invited me. It was the first time in what felt like forever that I decided to step away from motherhood for almost an entire day, to do something just for me. I showed up, a little flustered, a little tired — but I showed up.

The room was alive with chatter and hugs that felt like old friends reconnecting, even if they'd only just met. And then, I felt it — a pull. Deep, unexplainable. Like life was whispering, *"There's more. What if life could feel lighter, fuller, different?"*

I watched women standing in their power, speaking boldly about their dreams without a hint of apology. The energy in the room was electrifying, full of possibility. I was wearing a shimmer-thread sweater that caught the light, a little reminder that style can fake energy better than coffee. And in that moment, it hit me: I hadn't just dressed for the event. I'd dressed for the woman I was becoming.

Here's a challenge for you: Think about one area in your life where you've been running on autopilot — and then take just one conscious step to show up differently.

That's when I realized: style isn't just about clothes. It's a signal. Even something as small as lipstick is a signal. A quiet invitation to step into a version of yourself that's waiting to be seen. It's why, when I work with women on their style now, I don't start by saying, *"Buy more stuff."* I begin by reminding them of who they already are — and we build from there.

Then came the thought that wouldn't leave me: *It doesn't have to be like this.* Not the exhaustion of motherhood that had drained me. Not the loneliness. Not even the quiet distance in my marriage I'd been too tired to name. I didn't yet know what "different" would look like, but I knew it wasn't this.

So, within a month I enrolled in BOOST, Luly's community. On the surface, it's all about business strategy — branding, marketing, scaling. But really? It's about emotional breakthroughs disguised as networking. Every month, Luly opens her home to us for masterminds, seating us around her dining table with cafecito in hand. The air buzzes with laughter, side conversations, and the kind of raw honesty that can't be faked.

One day, sitting at her table, I saw something Luly had probably known all along: I have a gift for making things beautiful. Whether it's through style, interiors, or graphic design, I've always had this quiet ability to curate and inspire — something I had already been doing for years through *Blame it on Mei.* I kept telling myself that graphic design had to be my "thing" because I had the degree, the MBA, the résumé. But Luly saw through that. She made me realize that beauty wasn't just a side talent; it was the thread running through everything I touched. It wasn't a fallback; it was my calling.

How often do we underestimate the beauty we already create in our own lives?

By November 2024, I stopped running from that truth and launched *Pixel Pink Design* — the space where all my worlds finally came together. A place where I help elevate outfits, spaces, and brand graphics using what women already own. It's all about making them feel cohesive, elevated, and unapologetically themselves. Was it terrifying? Absolutely. But also freeing. It felt like a breadcrumb trail leading me back to the truth I'd always known: beauty matters. Not because of how it looks, but because of how it makes you feel.

From Spark to Luly's table, and then, in the most unexpected way, to my living room floor — that's where I realized one of life's most profound lessons. My son, Julian, wasn't just here for me to mother. He was here to teach me. His meltdowns, his endless *"why's,"* his unfiltered honesty — all of it forced me to confront the parts of myself I'd been avoiding. He was my mirror.

And then there was my daughter, Mila. Tutu over leggings, sparkly clips in her hair, with a look that said, *"I wear this because I love it."* No explanations, just pure, unapologetic joy in what she chose. Those glittery clips weren't just accessories; they were her crowns. Isn't that the kind of freedom I've always wanted? If I want her to grow up confident, unashamed of who she is, I have to show her what that looks like. Not just teach it. Live it.

One afternoon, amidst yet another storm of chaos, I felt it: the weight of trying to hold everything together—for him, for her, for my marriage, for my business. And instead of breaking, I whispered to myself: *"I am peace. I am love. I am patience."* Not because I believed it yet, but because I needed to. And in that fragile breath, something began to shift.

That was the moment when the layers started to fall into place. One day, the outfit of my life no longer looked like survival. It began to look like awakening. Because style, space, and self-expression aren't just frivolous, they're reflections of who you can become when you reclaim your life.

Where is the flicker of "more" in your life trying to get your attention right now?

CHOOSING ME, STYLING LIFE

Awareness is one thing. Living differently is another.

When I turned 42 — on the 24th, a mirrored number — it felt like a sign. A nudge to stop only reflecting on who I'd been and start stepping unapologetically into who I was becoming.

That year, I dove deeper into the resources from Luly's BOOST community. One of the BOOST sisters introduced me to the PRINT assessment. Seeing "perfectionism" spelled out in black and white wasn't shocking — it felt oddly familiar.

But I wasn't after another label. I needed a reckoning. And that's when Luly, along with my therapist, gently guided me toward another BOOSTIE: Adrianna Foster and her LOUD Women Nation, an immersive program dedicated to educating, empowering, and inspiring women through the power of authenticity.

Enter Adrianna. Her workshops didn't just hand out answers — they cracked you wide open. In one exercise, I had to imagine being in a plane crash, on my way home to see my family, and decide who would survive. I saved everyone — an entrepreneur, a woman with a troubled past, a mom of three. But when it came to me? I didn't save myself. Just like that. Gone.

The gut punch wasn't the crash — it was the clarity: even in my own mind, I chose everyone else over *me*.

It was in another exercise that I came across my shadow self: *"Perfect Betty."* The one with the clipboard, grading every little thing I did. But instead of just seeing her as the enemy, I felt a strange recognition — she was proof of what my PRINT assessment had already named in me. Perfectionism wasn't new; it had always been there, woven into everything I touched. The awakening was realizing she wasn't there to break me. She was there to show me something. Perfectionism, when I channeled it right, didn't have to be a cage. It could be a tool, something that worked *for* me instead of smothering me.

Take a moment today to reflect on one place where you're holding yourself to an impossible standard. And give yourself permission to release it.

Perfectionism didn't just show up in my work. It crept into every part of my life — especially my marriage. I became the keeper of everything: managing the kids' schedules, staying on top of endless WhatsApp school chats, handling the home's finances, and still trying to be the emotional sponge for my husband. I was beyond exhausted — a wife who felt more like a mother. And then, one day, the words tumbled out: "I am not your mother." Because deep down, I knew it was true. That's exactly what I had become.

Have you ever felt that? The bone-deep weariness of trying to be everything for everyone, while no one even notices how much you're falling apart?

Styling was my lifeline through it all. It stopped being just about clothes; it became my act of rebellion, my declaration of independence, and my path back to who I truly was. Every step I took in those heels was a reminder that I could rise above the hardest moments. The dress I wore for my 42nd birthday wasn't just a choice; it was a symbol of the joy I was reclaiming — proof that I could sparkle again.

But it was my community — Luly, especially — who helped me confront something I'd been running from for years: styling isn't just a hobby or a side gig for me. It's my passion. Not graphic design, even though that's where my degree and experience were. No, styling is where my true magic lives.

Blame it on Mei may have opened the door, but *Pixel Pink Design* became the room I finally allowed myself to step into fully. It wasn't just another business venture. It was the first time I allowed all parts of me to merge: the graphic designer, the stylist, the curator of spaces. *Pixel Pink Design* wasn't just a brand; it was where design and style came together, and where I finally felt at home.

Motherhood hasn't come to an end. Marriage hasn't miraculously fixed itself. Life still throws tantrums — sometimes from the kids, sometimes from me. But I no longer apologize for wanting more. For choosing myself. For showing up in spaces, in clothes, in a brand that finally reflects me.

And now, I turn to you. If you've ever looked in the mirror and wondered, *where did she go?* — this is for you. Through *Pixel Pink Design*, I help women do what I had to learn to do myself: find her again. Not by buying more. Not by starting over. But by elevating what's already there — in your closet, in your home, in your brand's graphics. Because unapologetic living isn't about accumulating more; it's about being more *you*.

The mirror won't bring her back. Choosing yourself will.

You don't have to wait for permission. You don't need a clean slate. You get to begin right here, right now. **What would change if, just for today, you chose yourself — unapologetically?**

About the Author

Once upon a time, my shoes clicked down corporate hallways. Today, they're more likely kicked off in a living room full of Legos. I'm Mei Jorge—a design curator, blogger, and mom of two who treats style as a power tool—for joy, self-expression, and showing up unapologetically.

After years in graphic design and marketing, I traded corporate deadlines for entrepreneurship, blending my love of aesthetics into *Pixel Pink Design* and my bilingual lifestyle blog, *Blame it on Mei*. Both have become playgrounds where I refine wardrobes, brand graphics, and spaces—using what's already there and making it shine.

In my chapter, I share how community helped me rediscover joy when life felt messy, marriage felt heavy, and motherhood overwhelming. Spoiler: the BOOST sisterhood reminded me I wasn't alone.

I hope my story inspires you to embrace your own beautifully imperfect journey—with bold lipstick optional, but highly recommended.

Find me on Instagram **@blameitonmei** explore more at **blameitonmei.com** or **pixelpinkdesign.com,** and scan the QR code for a special gift.

Chapter 9

FROM CHALKBOARD TO PASSPORT: WOMEN ENTREPRENEURS UNITE

BY SHANNON SUMMERVILLE-INTERIAN

Here's the story of a teacher who traded lesson plans for passports and freedom.

But how did I get here?

I ask myself this question often, especially on those drives home after another coworking day with Luly. The past six months have been a blur of change and new beginnings, and sometimes it still feels unreal. The mornings are always the same: up early, kids dropped off at school by 7:30am, a quick change of clothes, and then back in the car, already exhausted before the day has even really started. By 3:30, I'm rushing again, this time to pick up the kids. And yet, somewhere in all this hustle, I catch myself smiling. I can't wait to get home and dive into the work that's been filling my heart and mind at Luly's Coworking days.

The truth? I'm here because I finally took a leap of faith. For years, I had this quiet itch inside me, a longing for more, but I never let myself pursue it. It felt safer to stay in my routine, to stay where I was needed. But somewhere along the way, I realized I wasn't just missing out on adventures; I was missing out on myself.

Now, I work from home. I control my schedule. I can say "yes" to field trips, to the first days of school, to those small moments I used to slip by unnoticed. The ones I'd always hoped for but never had the time to truly experience.

For two decades, I taught in classrooms. I loved my students, but teaching was never my dream. It was safe. It was steady. But it wasn't me. I was going through the motions, convincing myself it was enough. Twenty-five years ago, I couldn't even imagine a life outside of teaching. But now? Now, I'm starting over; with clarity, with courage, and with the thrill of finally stepping into the life I was meant for.

So how did I end up a teacher if it wasn't my true calling or what I wanted? My senior year of high school looked nothing like I imagined. Instead of carefree weekends and senior trips, I was helping my dad care for my mom as she fought advanced cancer. My days were split between school, work, and taking care of her. I still wanted to be with my friends and my boyfriend, but deep down, I didn't fully understand how serious her illness was, until it was too late.

My graduation gift was supposed to be a trip to Europe to visit with my aunt. But as my mom's health worsened, that dream was put on hold as my mom's health declined. Before she passed, my mother asked me for only two things: to graduate from college and to travel the world. She had raised my brother at just fifteen, so for me, exploring the world wasn't just a dream, it was a promise I owed her. Just a few months after graduation, in 1996, she passed away. I was only 18.

I tried to start college that year, but I was too lost and broken to focus. That following spring, my father sent me on my graduation gift, a one-way ticket to Belgium. Being in a new country gave me a peace I hadn't felt in years. Everywhere I went, I felt my mother's presence. Travel gave me hope, and soon, I was sharing that passion with my girlfriends—planning affordable trips across Europe. It became our routine for the next several years.

Eventually, my dad said to me, "You love to travel, you love the arts—why not combine them and teach art?" It sounded like the safest, most stable and practical path: summers off, a pension, and still the freedom to travel. It was practical, and so, I followed it. Over the next 30 years, travel became my promise, my escape, and my lifeline. I traveled as far and wide as I could—taking part in a study abroad program in China. Teaching was rewarding. It gave me structure, purpose, and a steady rhythm. It was fun. I even led students on a summer trip to Italy and Greece. I built a career, earned recognition, and was even honored with Teacher of the Year in 2024.

But as fulfilling and safe as all that seemed, deep down, I always knew teaching wasn't born from true passion. It wasn't born from love or excitement, it came from a place of survival, of sadness, of trying to please others. I wanted to make my father proud, to show him that I could build a stable, solid life for myself. It was my way of reassuring him, and myself, that I was okay.

In the spring of 1997, I went on my European graduation gift trip. Toward the end of my journey, my dad and my youngest brother were supposed to join me, but in the end, only my dad came.

Those few weeks spent traveling together are moments I'll cherish forever. It felt special to share those experiences with him, even though I missed my brother terribly.

Then that fall, just weeks after we returned home, my world fell apart again. On my way to college, I found my brother. He had overdosed. It had only been ten months since my mother's death, and I couldn't wrap my mind around it. My father, who had always been my pillar of strength, was shattered. And I lost not only my brother but my best friend. That day, something inside of me died too.

The years that followed felt hollow. Holidays became a reminder of what we'd lost—unbearable. My father and I carried our grief like lead weights, barely managing to survive. We slept through the days, clinging to therapy no one else seemed to understand. We hadn't even begun to heal from the first loss when another struck.

Life marched on, though. I became a mother, something that should have been filled with pure joy. But every milestone with my children was clouded by the thought of my father losing his own child. In 2012, just as I was finding my footing, gaining balance in married life and raising a toddler, my oldest brother was diagnosed with cancer. He passed at the same age as our mother—53. Once again, I watched my father bury a child.

By 2018, I thought we had endured more than enough. But fate had other plans as tragedy struck again. My father buried his last living son. My brother, unable to survive the weight of his grief, was gone. Then, my uncle—who had always been like a second father to me—passed away. And as if that wasn't enough, my father's wife, now remarried, suffered three aneurysms, leaving her bedridden and completely dependent. My father, already broken, poured everything he had into caring for her. But the strain became too much. In 2022, he drank himself to death.

For the first time, I was left with only myself. No parents. No siblings. A strange, mixed feeling of devastation and release swept over me. I wasn't carrying my father's sadness anymore, but I had no idea who I was without it. At 45, I found myself asking: Who am I, after all of this?

There's always been this heaviness around my family. Simple questions like, "Do you have siblings?" or "What do your parents do?" felt impossible to answer. It was easier to say I was an only child or maybe even adopted than to dive into the painful truth of my losses and watch others squirm uncomfortably. For so long, I believed I was defined by my story—like that's all I had to offer, but deep down, I didn't want to keep living in it.

I spent years buried in grief, hiding in its shadow. But now? I'm done with that. I want to reinvent myself—not as someone stuck in the past, or as a victim of loss, but as someone who's finally free to chase the things that make me feel truly happy and alive.

People said I was running away. That my constant traveling was just a way to avoid facing reality. But they didn't get it. Every second of every day, my family was on my mind. Traveling didn't erase my grief, it expanded it. Suddenly, it wasn't just about me anymore. I was looking out at the world, and even in my sadness, I found peace. At eighteen, I knew this was the life I was meant to live. I just thought it would be something I'd have to wait for, maybe until I was old enough to retire.

When my father passed away, I bought a house in Italy. It wasn't some plan for my retirement; it was a gift. A gift I wanted to share with the people I loved. I wanted them to experience life the way I had started to see it: through moments of beauty, even when sadness loomed close. And it worked. They started visiting. And before long,

I found myself planning their flights, trains, excursions, weekends, all of it. The teacher in me came alive: hours of research, puzzles to solve, rabbit holes to dive into, all to create the perfect experience for them. What started as a passion project organically grew into a new career.

I started to think about my life differently. I owed it to my mom, my siblings, and I wanted to make my dad proud.

In 2023, I found myself torn. School had started, and I was caught between two worlds—teaching by day and booking travel by night. But inside that classroom, I felt suffocated. The pressure only grew when my daughter was diagnosed with epilepsy. She needed me, especially for the overnight school trips, but I couldn't be there because I didn't have the vacation hours. It became painfully clear: I couldn't keep chasing my dream of travel planning while stuck in a full-time job.

And in the back of my mind, I could hear my dad's voice: stability, your pension, your family—what are you doing? Was I being reckless? Then, in the middle of all the chaos, something unexpected happened—I was nominated and won Teacher of the Year. If anyone was confused, it was me.

In January, I accepted the Teacher of the Year award. By February, I walked into my principal's office, handed her my resignation papers, and told her I'd finish out the year, but I was leaving in June. She asked me to think it over, but I already knew. I was done. She even told me she admired my bravery.

So, I resigned. No backup plan, just the gut-deep certainty that I needed freedom, happiness, and the courage to follow my heart.

Here's the truth: I had no idea what I was doing. When school ended in June, I had just two clients. But this wasn't about the money. It was about freedom. It was about discovering who I really was. I'd never seen myself as a businesswoman, but suddenly, I was an entrepreneur. I didn't even fully understand what that meant. But what I knew was this: the only way to make it work was to jump—no safety net—and give it everything I had, even if it meant hitting rock bottom.

Earlier that year, I met Luly at a networking event I had nervously attended by myself. It was my first time stepping into a room full of entrepreneurs and business owners. I felt like an outsider, but we exchanged emails. Months later, she invited me to something called SPARK. I hadn't heard of it, but one of the sponsors was a familiar face, so I figured, why not? It's not like I was swamped with clients.

I walked in unsure of what to expect. I sat at the back, alone, clutching my notebook like it was some kind of shield. Slowly, though, I started recognizing a few familiar faces, and then the stories began. One by one, these women stood up and shared their journeys. A CEO who had left the corporate world to start fresh on her own. A chef who took the leap and went rogue. A finance professional who opened her own firm. None of their industries were anything like mine, yet their words struck me deep in the heart.

They all carried that same hunger I'd felt for so long: the longing for more. More freedom. More authenticity. More life. They didn't always have the answers, but they had the courage to step into the unknown. And in their stories, I saw myself.

When I walked out that night, my head was spinning. I knew I'd found my tribe. These women understood. They read my thoughts like reading from a book. Their words gave me excitement and a sense of empowerment I couldn't wait to share with anyone. I wanted to be everyone's friend, to soak up their wisdom, to finally feel like I belonged somewhere new.

But then came the hard part—speaking. I could stand in front of a room full of kids and command attention, but talking to adults? That terrified me. Elevator pitch? Thirty seconds? I froze. For the first time, I felt like the insecure one. And then, quietly, I told myself: No one's holding your hand here. Toughen up, buttercup. This is your new classroom.

I spent nearly 20 years teaching in the school system, holding an education degree, but none of that prepared me for what came next. I didn't know the first thing about being a salesperson, an accountant, or a boss. How could I? Suddenly, I was supposed to work for myself. Where do I even begin? I didn't have the luxury of time to go back to school, and now I was supposed to juggle and understand clients, marketing, social media, and still be the mom my kids needed.

That's when I found Luly's BOOST community, a group of women, all figuring out and navigating new paths. Some hadn't even started their businesses yet, while others, in their 50s, were launching second careers after years of being CEOs. These women inspired me, but I still found myself asking, where do I fit in? I had already started my business and had a few clients, but I wasn't looking for more business. I was craving something deeper, authenticity. A space where I could share ideas with women who truly understood the struggles. I wanted to grow, to be a better version of myself, and I knew that being part of this community could help me do that. And you can't put a price on that.

Family is great. They're supportive and loving, but their feedback is often gentle, too soft. What I needed was honesty. And that's exactly what I found here. Even on coworking days when I had no deadlines looming, just being in a room full of creativity and hearing women share ideas, it reminded me that I had something to offer too.

This community became more than just a support network. It became a lifeline. Almost a year in, I realized my whole perspective had changed. I wasn't just a travel agent anymore, booking flights and hotels. I had evolved into a concierge—crafting experiences, anticipating needs, ensuring every detail was perfectly aligned. I wasn't just sending people on vacations; I was creating memories, changing lives, just like travel had changed mine.

Without this community, I never would've seen my own potential so clearly. Luly's BOOST reminded me that I wasn't just booking travel. I was helping people build legacies.

If you're reading this and you're a woman in your 40s, juggling children, family, and all the other responsibilities that come with life, I need you to hear me loud and clear: life is too short to keep waiting for "someday." I spent years doing what I thought was the "right thing"—playing it safe, choosing stability, and always putting everyone else first. But deep down, I always knew there was more waiting for me. Not more money, not more recognition, but more life.

My journey has been filled with loss, but also with resilience. What saved me wasn't playing it safe—it was finding the courage to step outside my comfort zone, building a community of women who had my back, and taking leaps even when I didn't have all the answers. I'm living proof that you don't need a perfect plan. You don't need to have it all figured out. What you need is to listen to that quiet voice inside those whispers: There's more for you.

The truth is, courage doesn't mean the fear goes away. I was scared, too. But it was the strength I found in my community that kept me moving forward. Each small step I took brought me closer to the life I had always dreamed of.

So, here's my elixir to you: surround yourself with the right support system, women or men who lift you up, give yourself permission to be brave, and stop waiting for the "perfect moment" to be happy. Be kind to yourself. Your children don't just need a mother who sacrifices everything for them, they need a mother who's alive, fulfilled, and free.

Don't wait. Your "someday" is now.

About the Author

Hi, I'm Shannon Summerville-Interian—educator, entrepreneur, and travel designer passionate about guiding others through meaningful journeys.

With a degree in Education and more than seventeen years of teaching in diverse classrooms, I developed skills in mentorship, empathy, and communication—skills I now bring to my work as the founder of **Dorian Destinations**, a boutique luxury travel company renowned for its white-glove, personalized service.

My expertise spans global itineraries, cross-cultural connection, and hospitality management.

In my chapter, I share how loss and reinvention led me to leave a secure career and create something new—an act of courage I hope inspires others to embrace possibility.

When I'm not crafting journeys, you'll find me exploring hidden gems around the world. Connect with me at www.doriandestinations.com.

Chapter 10

GOING AT YOUR OWN PACE: FOR THE WOMAN WHO FEELS BEHIND BUT IS RIGHT ON TIME

BY CAROLINE DE POSADA

FOR THE WOMAN WHO FEELS BEHIND BUT IS RIGHT ON TIME

It was a Tuesday morning in 2014, and I had taken the day off work to do the thing I loved most: watch my father speak. Michelle Villalobos was hosting a women's event in Miami, and my father was the keynote speaker. Normally, I sat alone, front and center, soaking up every word as I watched him on stage. But today, something was different.

As I scanned the room, my eyes landed on a familiar face.

Luly B. A woman I had known since high school.

Her presence caught me off guard. I wasn't used to seeing anyone from my "Miami" life at these types of events.

But there she was, smiling and shining.

When I walked up to hug her and ask what brought her to the event, I learned that Luly had stepped into my father's world. She had created a brand called *Balance is Bullshit* and was speaking all over the country. I was thrilled for Luly. But it also triggered something I wasn't expecting.

Sadness? Jealousy? Maybe even desire?

I couldn't quite name it. Deep down, there was always a part of me that longed to do the work my father did… and to do it *with* him. But I always had a reason to hold back.

At seventeen, I told myself I was too young to be a motivational speaker. *How can I tell people how to live their lives when I haven't even lived mine?*

My father would gently push back, saying, "Caro, you've been through more in your 17 years than you realize, my love. You could help so many people." But I couldn't see it.

By twenty-five, my path looked very different. I was busy keeping the promise I had made to my grandfather: to become a lawyer. People always said I had wanted to be a lawyer since I was five years old, and that story followed me my whole life.

Going at Your Own Pace:
For the Woman Who Feels Behind but Is Right on Time

For my grandfather, it was more than a dream; it was a source of pride. He had been a lawyer in Cuba, and then, at forty-seven, started all over again in the United States, learning English as a second language and earning his law degree a second time. In a Cuban family, becoming a lawyer was one of the highest achievements imaginable. My grandfather had done it twice, and his deepest wish was to see his granddaughter follow in his footsteps. I wanted to keep that promise. So, I did.

By thirty, I was married and had my first baby. I had grown up in the middle of divorce. Between both of my parents, there were nine divorces altogether. On top of that, my father spent nearly eighty percent of his time traveling for speaking engagements. He was a wonderful father, but his career and lifestyle didn't seem to foster a traditional family life. The one who was there every single day was my wonderful mother. I came to believe I couldn't have both my father's career and a stable family. I wanted the family more.

Those beliefs buried my dream of speaking alongside my father so deeply that I almost forgot I had ever dreamed it. But here I was at thirty-five, and this unexpected encounter with this woman from my youth had unlocked something inside me. She, too, was a wife and a mother, about my age, and yet she was doing the very thing I had deemed impossible.

The tangled feelings I felt that day weren't only because Luly was living this life and I wasn't. It was heavier than that. I was also carrying a secret no one else in that room knew. My father was dying. And I knew my window to work beside him (that desire I had buried and ignored for so long) was closing faster than I could bear.

A year later, I sat at my father's deathbed, holding his hands in mine, leaning close so my face

was right next to his. All through his illness, we had faced every step calmly, honestly, and stoically. Yet in this moment, tears, fears, and everything I'd managed to keep steady before suddenly poured out of me.

"Dad," I whispered, my voice shaking, "I don't know how to live without you in my life."

He wasn't just my father. He was my mentor, my best friend, my soul mate. He had always been my person. "And your world…" I added through tears. "The events you take me to, NSA, everything you're always learning. I don't know how to find any of it without you." My dad reached up to wipe the tears off my face, and smiled softly. "Oh, mi amor," he said, "you don't have to worry about that. That world will find you. It's part of your destiny."

On June 11, 2015, I said goodbye to my father for the last time. That day, I made a promise to carry his legacy forward. I just didn't know how. A couple of months later, I received a message from Luly B. She offered her condolences and asked if there was anything she could do. I asked her to meet me for lunch.

Going at Your Own Pace:
For the Woman Who Feels Behind but Is Right on Time

We met at The Cheese Course. She was waiting for me at a small table by the window. I had gone there intending to pick her brain about her speaking career. But things didn't go as planned. From the moment I greeted her, all I could do was cry.

Earlier that year, Luly had started a coaching community called Boost. But she didn't try to sell me on it. Instead, she simply shared a meal with me, offered a few words of encouragement, and, most importantly, gave me the quiet space to hold me and my tears. By the end of that lunch, I knew she was someone I could trust. If I had known then what I know now, I would have joined Boost on the spot. But I was still caught in grief, uncertainty, some money mindset issues, and worst of all… paralysis by analysis.

I had grown up so entrenched in the personal development and speaking world with my father that in many ways I was an expert. I wore that expertise like a badge of honor, not realizing it had become armor that imprisoned my spirit.

Because sometimes the problem isn't what you don't know. The problem is what you think you know that keeps you from learning what you don't.

During that same season of my life, I was training for a marathon with my soul sister, Betsy Guerra (one of the co-authors of this book). Week after week, as we pounded the pavement, we talked about everything under the sun.

I often shared stories about my father, his work, and the speaking profession. One day, Betsy said, "I want to be a speaker." The next day, she joined Boost. That's Betsy ... bold, fast-moving, and a true go-getter. Me? I was more like a turtle.

It would take me another full year before I finally joined Luly's community in 2018. I still remember sitting at Luly's kitchen table, feeling like I was the only one who couldn't quite figure things out.

I wanted to speak, but I didn't want to travel.

I wanted to inspire the world, but I wasn't even sure who "the world" was.

I wanted to follow in my dad's footsteps, but his shoes felt too big to fill, and the path he had paved felt too far from home. Luly told me I'd make an incredible coach. I laughed. She also told me I was an inspirational storyteller. And all I could think was, Great, but who's going to pay me to be an inspirational storyteller? One day during our mastermind, after I poured out how stuck I felt, Luly gave me a piece of homework: "Be still."

Her suggestion infuriated me. Be still? Wasn't doing nothing already my specialty? For years, I felt small, uncertain, and slow. *So very slow*. I watched the women around me gaining speed, catching momentum, while I chugged along ... like a *turtle*.

And yet, looking back now, those weren't wasted years. I spent my days raising my three boys and savoring every minute; I worked on healing my marriage while mending the deep wound of losing my dad. I even wrote a book I was so proud of, titled *Looking Over the Edge: Facing Your Fears, Finding Your Way, and All the Lessons in*

Between. I blogged consistently. I developed a framework called CORE, and occasionally spoke about it for companies, organizations, and associations.

I was living out my principles in my personal life, applying my beliefs and frameworks every day yet I still carried the weight of not feeling like I was doing enough.

And then, within three months, life stopped me in my tracks. I suffered a life-threatening pneumonia that landed me in the ICU for a week. Then, COVID hit. Those two experiences did something for me I didn't know I needed: they got me out of my head and back into my heart.

I stopped obsessing over whether I was good enough, fast enough, or smart enough. I began to see my real limitation: I had been terrified of doing things wrong, making a mistake, or looking like an amateur. Deep down, I knew why. My heroes (my father and his friends) seemed so much larger than life that I felt I'd never measure up. But in that season, I received the clearest message: it was game-time. And my only job was to serve as best as I could. So during those COVID days, when the world was isolated and stuck at home, I began showing up live on Instagram every night of the week to share words of encouragement, practical tools, and personal stories. Without realizing it, I was already coaching. I was already telling stories meant to inspire.

I wasn't getting paid for it but that didn't matter. All I cared about was serving. In the middle of COVID, I invited anyone who wanted to join me for a plank challenge. To my surprise, fifty women signed up.

Through that experience, I discovered something important: what these women really needed was to *start with CORE.* That spontaneous idea turned into 28-day CORE challenges, which went on to serve more than 350 women; many of them the same Boosties I had once sat beside at Luly's kitchen table, back when I had no idea where my new career was headed. The more I showed up and served, the clearer the path became, and suddenly I had transitioned from lawyer to life coach doing most of my work through *inspirational storytelling.*

Over the last six years, I've continued to expand my work. Today, I guide high-achieving humans to Live with Intention, using signature tools like CORE and DARE to build strong foundations, take aligned action, and create daily rhythms that support a bliss-full life. These methods were born from my own journey of healing, clarity, and courage. And it all started at Luly's kitchen table.

Here's the thing about the messy middle that no one tells you: one step at a time doesn't feel like much until you look back and realize you've walked a thousand miles.

Today, Luly, Betsy, and I have created what we call a trifecta effect. We are each other's teachers, students, and collaborators. We weave in and out of each other's lives and businesses with faith, love, friendship, and profound service. Together, we have built something greater than any of us could have built on our own ... *a sisterhood.*

My father was right.

His world, the one I was so afraid of losing, didn't disappear. It found me. But the truth is, it found me long before that conversation at his deathbed. It found me the day I ran into Luly at that personal development conference back in 2014. Those emotions I felt that day? That was the Universe nudging me, preparing me, training me for something bigger. And I know Luly was meant to be part of that plan. I will forever be grateful to her for having the courage to build a business and a community that supports women like me. Because what started as a *boost* eventually led me to find my *bliss.*

Bliss is within you. It can't be faked or forced. It already lives inside you. It's born in alignment when who you are, what you believe, and how you live are finally in harmony. But here's the thing: no one else can tell you how fast or slow your path should be. Trust the process. Keep moving forward. And when you grow weary, lean on the shoulders of the trailblazers who were brave enough to begin before you. So, whether you need a boost… or you're ready to Bliss'n Up… remember this: you don't have to walk through the messy middle alone.

When you're ready to step from Boost to Bliss, our communities will be here, waiting to walk with you.

About the Author

Hi, I'm Caro de Posada, a lawyer-turned-life-coach, inspirational storyteller, wife, and mom on a mission to help people unlock bliss.

As a coach, speaker, author, and host of the *Bliss'n Up Podcast*, I've spent the last decade guiding individuals and couples to elevate their mindset, wellness, and relationships so they can thrive both personally and professionally.

In this chapter, you'll discover how community, courage, and small steps can move you beyond self-doubt into clarity, confidence, and a more aligned path.

When I'm not working, you'll likely find me on a sunrise walk with friends, piecing together a jigsaw puzzle, or navigating the joyful chaos of life as a wife and mom of three boys.

My hope is that my story encourages you to trust your timing, honor your path, and keep moving forward—one small step at a time. You can follow my journey on Instagram **@carolinedeposada** or connect with me at **carolinedeposada.com/coaching**.

Give Me A Boost

ACKNOWLEDGEMENTS

To my parents, Maru and Jr.:

You gave me my very first BOOST and never stopped cheering on your relentless little girl. Your unwavering belief, unconditional love, and steady support have been the source of my strength and recharge throughout my life.

To the men of my life; my husband, Gino, and my sons, George and Marcelo:

Thank you for embracing my light and celebrating all of who I am. Your love and support mean the world to me. May the way you see, honor, and champion me be an inspiration for other men walking alongside powerful, brave women.

To our book coach & publisher, Sandra Rodriguez Bicknell:

Thank you from the bottom of my heart for your support and guidance throughout this journey. Your grace and ability to help us bring this book to life on such a tight timeline made it possible to celebrate the 10th anniversary of BOOST in the most meaningful way. This dream became a reality because of you, and I am forever grateful.

To the remarkable women who co-authored this book: Barbie, Betsy, Caro, Daniela, Eva, Gilza, Luly, Maitte, Mei, Shannon:

Thank you for saying yes to this beautiful project, which will be an enormous gift to so many! Thank you for showing up with such bravery and authenticity. Your breakthroughs are a testament to the power of saying YES to yourself and to community.

To the BOOST community:

To the hundreds of women who said yes to BOOST since 2015, thank you for your love and grace through the ups and downs of this community and of my own life. You carried me through the darkest seasons and celebrated with me in the brightest ones.

Together, we've lived so much: welcoming babies and grandbabies, becoming bird launchers, watching our children get married, saying goodbye to loved ones, experiencing divorce, and even cheering on a son as he became a Marine. We've transitioned careers, left jobs, launched businesses, and shifted old ones into new. We've sought support for our children, our marriages, and our dreams. We've grown deeper in our spirituality and stronger in our wellness.

And through it all, we have proven something powerful: there can be a sacred space where women grow in every aspect of their lives, where we can speak our truth in business and in life. A space where we don't compete, but instead collaborate and celebrate one another.

Acknowledgements

You are living proof that when we gather, we rise. And in rising, we've become not just a community, but an example and an inspiration to the world.

Give Me A Boost

THANK YOU

From my heart to yours, thank you for holding this book in your hands and allowing the words within it to touch your spirit. Every story shared here was written with courage, vulnerability, and love, and it is our hope that you feel seen, inspired, and uplifted through these pages.

As a BOOSTIE myself, this project is deeply personal. I know firsthand the power of this sisterhood and the way it calls us to rise higher, together. Being able to walk alongside these incredible women and with Luly, whose vision and heart created BOOST, as their coach and publisher has been both an honor and a blessing.

Thank you for saying "yes" to this journey with us. By reading, you've become part of BOOST in your own way, a living thread woven into the fabric of courage, connection, and growth. May what you've discovered here continue to echo in your own life and ripple out into the lives of others.

With gratitude and love,
Sandra Rodriguez Bicknell
Publisher, Coach, and Fellow BOOSTIE.

Give Me A Boost

GET YOUR BOOST

Hey there, Fabulous!

My hope is that this book reminded you of what's possible when you stop doing it alone and start saying yes to the BOOST. Perhaps you saw a piece of yourself in our stories, and something inside you whispered, "I can do this too."

Let's keep this conversation going! I'd love to cheer you on, share tools, and support you in building a business and life of significance. Just scan the QR code below to grab instant access to bonus content and join the community of women who are saying YES to the BOOST!

XO,

Click to join the community and get BONUS content!

www.WomenWhoBoost.com

www.ingramcontent.com/pod-product-compliance
Lightning Source LLC
Chambersburg PA
CBHW062225080426
42734CB00010B/2024